THE HOLINESS EXPERIENCE —AND ITS— EVOLUTION

GEORGE A. MILLER

Copyright © 2024 George A. Miller.

All rights reserved. No part of this book may be reproduced, stored, or transmitted by any means—whether auditory, graphic, mechanical, or electronic—without written permission of both publisher and author, except in the case of brief excerpts used in critical articles and reviews. Unauthorized reproduction of any part of this work is illegal and is punishable by law.

ISBN: 979-8-89031-859-6 (sc)
ISBN: 979-8-89031-860-2 (hc)
ISBN: 979-8-89031-861-9 (e)

Library of Congress Catalog Card Number: 2005901945

Because of the dynamic nature of the Internet, any web addresses or links contained in this book may have changed since publication and may no longer be valid. The views expressed in this work are solely those of the author and do not necessarily reflect the views of the publisher, and the publisher hereby disclaims any responsibility for them.

One Galleria Blvd., Suite 1900, Metairie, LA 70001
(504) 702-6708

DEDICATION

This book is dedicated to my former pastor and friend the late Elder J.T. Hill

CONTENTS

Acknowledgements vii
Foreword ix

Chapter 1 Introduction 1

Chapter 2 The Theology of Holiness Thought 9
The Protestant Principle 10
Origin of the Holiness Movement 12
Holiness and the African American Experience 24

**Chapter 3 Doctrinal Sues that Created
            New Schools of Thought** 29
Moving Beyond Methodism 30
Entire Sanctification 31
Conflicting Views Regarding Holiness Teaching 37
The Gift of the Holy Spirit 41

**Chapter 4 Pentecostalism: In Offshoot of the
            Holiness Movement** 45
Pre-pentecostal History 51
The History of Pentecostalism 53
The Pentecostal Holiness Church 54
Diversification of Denominational Adherents 55

Chapter 5 Major Contributions of the Holiness Faith 66
Deepening of Spritual Life 67
The Establishment of Religious Organizations 68
Moral and Spiritual Implications 74

Chapter 6 The Hand of God that Direct Religious History 77

Protestant Theology and God's Intervention 78
Pentecostal Theology and Spiritual Gifts 82
The Unity of Holiness and Pentecostal Doctrine 88

Summary & Conclusion 101
Endnotes 107
Bibliography 111

ACKNOWLEDGEMENTS

I want to express my appreciation to the many people who contributed their time and effort in the furtherance of this study. I am especially indebted to Dr. Wanda Stallings, whose wise guidance and counsel has been a constant source of encouragement. The employees of Mississippi State University Library offered valuable advice in locating needed resource materials. Their interest and consideration was crucial to the completion of the research project. The cooperation and understanding of my family provided valuable help as I met the challenge of the investigation.

FOREWORD

The purpose of this book is to highlight major contributions that the Holiness Movement brought to the Christian faith. The literature establishes the Holiness Movement as the catalyst that led the way for religious change in America. The study of The Holiness Experience and Its Evolution will inspire Christians to embrace the Holiness message. Such a decision will serve to strengthen our appreciation for God's mandate to live a Holy life. When we observe this biblical truth affirmed and see it declared by our spiritual leaders, it should provide an opportunity for us to achieve new zeal in renewing our commitment to the teaching, preaching, and obedience to God's Holy Word. Ultimately, living out that commitment in the church and community will be determined by personal commitment. It is my prayer that while reading this study, God will manifest Himself in our hearts and minds, and thus create a passion for the promise of hope that is found in living the Holy life. It is also my desire that this investigation will generate a revival within Holiness movements everywhere, bring-ins a powerful move of God upon all Christendom.

Readers will find the study interesting and informative. Readers will be enlightened and informed in religious doctrine and historical events that occurred during the early nineteenth century. Readers should discover how these events led to religious stratification among church organizations. Readers should search their hearts as they examine doctrinal issues that created division among the family of God. The study will reveal important facts that will drastically diminish debatable issues between religious leaders.

Believers should combine as one army and accept the truth found in God's word. Although there are many administrations, there is but one Lord over all:

"One faith, one Lord and one baptism." Believers can be drawn closer together as they understand that we are God's children and He commands every believer to embrace the Holy life.

It is evident that the Holiness experience was a movement inspired by God. The phenomenon changed the face of religious history forever. Readers must understand that it is the hand of God that directs religious history. The emergence of the Holiness experience was not by chance. God used this platform not only to expand the work of the kingdom but also to reach millions with the message of a heavenly hope.

Readers will recognize the apparent fact that the state of Christendom is divided. We are all too well aware of the hundreds of religious groups that cluster themselves under separate religious agendas. Indeed, they are not only willing, but also proud to embrace teaching that separates them from other Christians. As a result of this research, readers will learn to appreciate the many differences found within the family of believers.

The knowledge obtained from completing this study allowed me to achieve a deeper understanding and appreciation of America's religious history. I discovered a strong correlation between Holiness and Pentecostal groups in the expansion of religious theology in America. Each religious group was made up of many diverse organizations, most of which are predominantly southern in membership and influence. The early Pentecostal church originated in the south, where Holiness Movements had swept the area for decades. In 1901, Charles Parham, a Kansas Holiness preacher, laid the doctrinal and experimental foundations of the modern Pentecostal Movement.

It was interesting to study the history of the Azusa experience because it was crucial to the stratification of many religious adherents. The Pentecostal Movement in America, for instance, evolved from the closely preceding Holiness Movement, which itself was established from the much earlier Wesleyan emphasis on experiencing Christian Perfection after redemption. At the end of the nineteenth century and the beginning of the twentieth, many individuals left established mainline religious organizations to escape what they perceived as liberalism and worldliness. The above aforementioned issues paved the way for religious stratification and caused a continual evolvement into a massive family that owes much of its foundation to Holiness and Pentecostal beliefs.

The doctrine of Entire Sanctification was a focal point for the establishment of the Holiness agenda. The expansion and teaching of Entire Sanctification would eventually bring about a division among believers. The division was not what John Wesley intended to accomplish while challenging his followers to pursue a higher calling in God. I view the teaching of John Wesley as the one of the main events that brought about issues that kindled the fire of indifference among Wesley's followers.

Wesley believed that sanctification is the work of the Holy Spirit by which the child of God is separated from sin unto God and is enabled to love God with all his heart and to walk blamelessly in all His Holy commandments. Sanctification is initiated at the moment of justification and regeneration. From that moment there is a gradual or progressive sanctification as the believer walks with

God and grows in grace and in a more perfect obedience to God. Entire Sanctification is an experience that is brought instantaneously when the believer presents himself as a living sacrifice, holy and acceptable to God, through faith in Jesus Christ. The believer is filled by the baptism with the Holy Spirit who cleanses the heart from all sin. The experience of Entire Sanctification perfects the believer in love and empowers him/her for effective service. It is followed by lifelong growth in grace and the knowledge of our Lord and Savior Jesus Christ. The life of holiness continues through faith in the sanctifying blood of Christ and evidences itself by loving obedience to God's will.

The breakout of Holiness revivals started in 1865. The Civil War left in its wake a moral and spiritual crisis that prominent Methodist pastors believed could be met only by a return to the faith of their founders. John C. McClintock, a leader for the cause of Christian Perfection led the way for other followers who embraced the teaching of Entire Sanctification. He declared that Christian perfection was the central theme to the Bible and the chief goal of Wesleyan piety. Such beliefs kindled the desire for church followers to seek a deeper understanding of God's love.

The study of the Holiness Movement provides overwhelming data, presenting the history that African Americans contributed to religious history. The importance of the relationship of African Americans to the Holiness Movement cannot be overlooked. Historical literature reveals that as early as 1887, the characteristics of African American worship in religious services had been noted. Given that the ultimate objective of worship in some Holiness church tradition is some form of spiritual manifestation, the aesthetic and ethical norms that govern movement toward this objective are derived from the Bible and black culture. The distinctive songs, speech, and dances of the Holiness church symbolically "usher" the saints "out" of this world and into a more authentic one discerned within sacred time and space. What makes this process exilic is the connection made between the saints' rejection of the world and the world's rejection of the saints.

A teaching common to all Holiness followers is the belief that human beings can live a life set apart for God. Holiness churches are united in the belief that Christians can approach freedom from sin during their earthly lives. In addition to one's baptism into the Christian faith, Holiness churches teach that the second blessing, a baptism of the Holy Spirit, makes perfect the Christian impulse toward moral sanctification. Strong belief in the power of the Holy Spirit often means that Holiness services are enthusiastic occasions for worship.

Readers will appreciate a clearer understanding regarding the gifts of the spirit and the gifts of tongues. Speaking in tongues is a phenomenon in which the believer, in an ecstatic state, speaks in a foreign language or utters unintelligible sounds that are taken to contain a divine message. Many Christians believe the genuine gifts of tongues were confined to earliest Christianity, at Pentecost, and during conversion experiences. Modern revivalist movements such as the Pentecostals and some Holiness followers believe it to be given in contemporary times as a testimony to the special presence of the Holy Spirit.

The study of the Holiness Movement and its evolution will provide a guide for diminishing religious indifference among church leadership and draw believers closer together across denominational lines. The impact will produce a better understanding of the many differences that exist among church organizations.

CHAPTER 1

INTRODUCTION

The Holiness Movement is the key that opened the door for the stratification of many religious beliefs that revolutionized the way mainline Christian followers applied biblical teaching. Holiness teaching paved the way for religious disciplines that impacted America. The platform established by Holiness explorers provided a springboard for the Pentecostal Movement and other religious organizations that came into existence during the nineteenth century. The Holiness Movement started as an effort to preserve and propagate John Wesley's teaching on Entire Sanctification and Christian Perfection.[1] According to Wesley, "The road from sin to salvation is one from willful rebellion against divine and human law to perfect love for God and man" (Pierard, 2001, pp. 1). Conflicting views regarding Holiness teaching contributed to doctrinal issues that were crucial in creating opposing religious theologies that would expand the growth of the Holiness Movement for decades to come.

Holiness followers emphasized that the process of salvation involves two theologies. First, in conversion or justification, man is freed from the sins he has com-mitted. Second, with Entire

Sanctification or full salvation, man is freed from the flaw in his moral nature that causes him to sin. Mankind can obtain perfection even though he dwells in an imperfect body marked by a thousand defects arising from ignorance, infirmities, and other human limitations. The Holiness Principle is a process of loving the Lord God with all of one's heart, soul, and mind, and it results in the ability to live with a conscience. According to Wesley, to achieve and then remain in this blessed state requires intense, sustained effort, and one's life must be marked by constant self renunciation; careful observance of the divine ordi-nances; a humble, steadfast reliance on God's forgiving grace in the atonement; the intention to look for God's glory in all things; and an increasing exercise of the love which fulfills the whole law and is the end of the commandments (Pierard, 2001).

The growth of the Holiness Movement created new schools of thought as Holiness doctrine impacted the religious community. In the mid-nineteenth century, several factors converged that contributed to the renewal of the Holiness emphasis: the camp meeting revivals that were a common feature in rural America, the Christian perfectionism of Charles Finney and Asa Mahan (the Oberlin theology), and protests within the Methodist churches about the decline of discipline which resulted in the Wesleyan Methodist secession in 1843 and the Free Methodist withdrawal in 1860.[2] These two became the first denominations formally committed to Holiness. After the Civil War, a full-fledged Holiness revival broke out within the ranks of Methodism, and in 1867 the National Camp Meeting Association for the Promotion of Holiness was formed. Camp meetings became the device that was used to encourage an evangelistic zeal that revolutionized the spiritual temper of rural America. The itinerant preachers were met with enthusiasm that welcomed the birth of camp meetings (Posey, 1933).

The camp meeting message was simple. Christ died for all people, and everyone who repented and believed would be saved. Preachers depicted the heavenly serenity waiting believers and the eternal torments nonbelievers would suffer. The camp meeting environment would be crucial in enhancing the zeal that would push the quest for religious experience to new levels (Owen, 1998).

The Holiness Movement's early self-understanding of its mission in relation to the existing churches also contributed to its "main-line" character. The Holiness revival in America was born in the 1830s out of the efforts of its Methodist founders to restore the experiential knowledge of Wesley's evangelical perfectionism to the central position that the doctrine traditionally had held in Methodism. At the same time, the Movement's conviction that the race of Christian Perfection, or Entire Sanctification, and the Baptism of the Holy Ghost were biblical and were to be the normal expectation of every believer's experience aroused a sense of evangelistic responsibility among its ardent advocates to spread their gospel of "Full Salvation" to Christians of every ecclesiological, theological, and social stripe. The extensive Arminianization of American religion prepared the field for a more ready acceptance of the Holiness revivalist's message among non-Methodist evangelicals than might otherwise have been possible.

Due to concerns regarding reform and renewal, for almost three generations most of the Movement remained loyal to the churches in which the revival arose, resisting the separatist tendencies that often accompany such renewal movements. A direct program or demand for the reformation of the accepted polity or orthodoxy of the churches was not part of the Holiness advocates' call for ethical and social reformation at that period. At its peak in 1875, the revival was a movement working wholly within the existing Methodist and non-Methodist Protestant churches in America, England, the remainder of Europe, and their missions extending around the world.

The National Holiness Association (NHA), the dominant agency of the revival, adamantly maintained its antiseparatist stance even in the face of the constantly increasing separatist pressures by thousands of newly acquired converts who had never joined any church. No one could be a member of one of the hundreds of county or state Holiness associations, who did not maintain good standing within one of the existing denominations. The National Association's leaders looked on with dismay as Daniel Warner and other early "come-outers" called for separate organizations "on the Holiness line" in the early 1880s.

It was not until the end of the century that large numbers of Methodists together with lesser numbers of Baptists, Presbyterians, and others reluctantly joined the earlier "come-outers." They organized such Holiness churches as The Pentecostal Church of the Nazarene, now the Church of the Nazarene, Church of God, and the Pilgrim Holiness Church, now part of the Wesleyan Church. Even then, the historic Methodist influences on the Movement remained strong through the involvement of the Free Methodist and the Wesleyan Methodist Churches, two smaller Methodist groups who were strongly committed to the revival.

Many other "friends of Holiness" walked the difficult path of continuing their allegiance to the Holiness Movement while remaining loyal to the older churches. These factors helped to maintain among Holiness adherents a sense of historical continuity with the traditional churches, even when more radical primitivist restitutionist themes came to the fore as the revival approached the end of the century. This factor goes a long way in explaining why the Holiness adherents tried to distinguish themselves so radically from their much more eschatologically oriented Pentecostal Movement siblings.

The Holiness Movement generally had seen itself as a movement growing out of the development of the historical church. In its historical and theological development, therefore, it is easy, as well as logical, to identify a pervasive Holiness tradition, one which seems to segregate it from the mainline religious groups.

An increasing number of Holiness evangelists un-sanctioned by their superiors, a flourishing independent press, and the growth of nondenominational associations gradually weakened the position of mainline Methodism in the movement. By the 1880s, the first independent Holiness denominations had begun to appear, and tensions between Methodism and the Holiness associations escalated. The gap between the two widened as Methodist practice drifted steadily toward a sedate, middleclass Protestantism, while the Holiness groups insisted they were the true successors of Wesley in America (Pierard, 2001).

The polity of these bodies was a modified Methodism in that there was generally somewhat more congregational autonomy, and the "second blessing" of Entire Sanctification was an integral part of their theology.[3] Generally they operated with a strict perfectionist code of personal morality and demanded from their adherent's plain dress and abstinence from "worldly" pleasures and amusements (Pierard, 2001).

The Holiness Movement quickly spread beyond the bounds of Methodism. A Mennonite group, the United Missionary Church (formerly Mennonite Brethren in Christ and since a merger in 1969 called the Missionary Church), adopted the doctrine of Entire Sanctification and Holiness standards of personal conduct. The Brethren in Christ (founded 1863) was of mixed Pennsylvania German Pietist and Mennonite origins, but it also took on Wesleyan Perfectionism. A meeting of the religious group Four Quaker, which had been influenced by Holiness doctrines, took place in 1947 to form the Evangelical Friends Alliance. The Salvation Army also has had a firm commitment to Holiness. The Christian and Missionary Alliance, with its emphasis on Christ as Savior, Sanctifier, Healer, and coming King, has an affinity with the Wesleyan movement, and its two most prominent thinkers, A.B. Simpson and A.W. Tozer, are widely read in Holiness circles, but the doctrine of the eradication of sin was never accepted (Pierard, 2001).

Holiness teaching was taught in African American Baptist churches in the 1800's. In 1894, a Baptist minister felt the need for a deeper revelation of God's will for his life. The pastor of Mount Helm Baptist Church in Jackson, Mississippi, Charles Price Jones, began to seek God with his whole heart for the power that would make his life wholly God's. As a result, conflict arose among the brothers. Followers of the Holiness doctrine were forced to separate themselves from the Baptist fellowship and form an organization that he called the Holiness Movement. The newly formed organization was considered independent for two decades. C. H. Mason was a strong preacher within the Holiness group and would eventually leave the group and later become the leader of one of the largest religious groups within this country, the Church of God in Christ. Both Jones and Mason were great administrators and prolific song writers. The Holiness group eventually became a denomination currently known as the Church of Christ Holiness U.S.A. Charles Price Jones was eventually named its leader and founder (Cobbins, 1966).

The growth of the independent churches was related to the decline of the Holiness emphasis within Method-ism, and after World War II denominationalism turned the originally evangelistic NHA into a council of Holiness churches. But numerical growth and material prosperity led inexorably to compromise with contemporary culture, and the relaxation of personal discipline was reflected in the wearing of fashionable dress and jewelry and secular entertainments such as participation in athletics and television viewing. As a result, several conservative splinter groups seceded from the Holiness denominations and joined together in an interchurch organization in 1947 known as the Interdenominational Holiness Convention. This group now sees itself as the defender of pristine Wesleyanism (Pierard, 2001).

Pentecostalism, which is an offshoot of the Holiness Movement, stresses that speaking in tongues is the evidence that one has received the second blessing. At a Bible school in Topeka, Kansas, founded by a Holiness evangelist, the "gift of the Spirit" came to a student in 1901, and the practice of glossolalia quickly spread. The Pentecostal revival made its greatest inroads in areas where Holiness movements were already prospering, and it attracted far more non-Methodists than had the earlier forms of perfectionism. Besides the emphasis on the baptism of the Holy Spirit, Pentecostalism recognized divine healing and demanded highly puritanical standards of personal conduct. Like the Holiness groups, the Pentecostals were theological conservatives, and they comprised an important addition to the Arminian wing of Protestant conservatism in the period when the Fundamentalist Movement was gathering steam. Some Holiness denominations, most notably the Church of the Nazarene, flatly reject the use of tongues, while others, such as the Pentecostal Holiness Church, teach both glossolalia and Entire Sanctification. Denominationalism soon took hold in Pentecostalism, and before long it had more adherents than its parent in such bodies as the Assemblies of God, the black Church of God in Christ, and the International Church of the Foursquare Gospel (Pierard, 2001).

The Holiness Movement contributed to a richer spiritual life in a materialistic age, and it was a necessary contrast to offset the sterile intellectualism and dead orthodoxy that characterized so many churches at the time. However, it has been criticized for suggesting that a "second blessing" can provide some Christians with a higher kind of sanctification than that which flows from one's justifying faith. Other objections include the tendency to identify Holiness with quietism self abasement and even loss of personality, an other-worldly asceticism that calls for the rejection of all secular culture as sinful, confining the grace of God to stereotyped forms of religious experience, an overemphasis on feeling, and claiming with overweening confidence the special action of the Holy Spirit in one's life and direct inspiration in the details of thought and action (Pierard, 2001).

The emergence of the Holiness Movement during the early nineteenth century was a catalyst that created controversial religious views that changed the direction of religious history forever and forged the establishment of various religious denominations throughout the United States and the world.

CHAPTER 2

THE THEOLOGY OF HOLINESS THOUGHT

In order to understand how the Holiness Movement evolved, there must be an understanding of Protestant theology. Protestant theology existed as the teaching of mainline religious groups. Mainline religious groups such as Methodist and Baptist believed that their faith was determined by the belief that believers are saved by grace through faith in Christ Jesus. Many Holiness followers support the fact that they are Protestant. Protestants embrace the convictions that give Protestantism its unique character among the branches of Christianity: salvation by grace alone through faith, the sole authority of Scripture for faith and practice, and the universal priesthood of believers. The American Holiness Movement identifies itself as theologically Protestant. In fact, Protestantism is not an option for the movement. It is an imperative. Further, it is hoped that it will be adequately demonstrated that it is precisely the Movement's doctrinal reason that dictates it be Protestant (Bassett, 2001).

The Protestant Principle

Believing its origin to be an expression of the Gospel, Protestantism accepts the entire history of the manifestation of the Gospel as its own history. It does not see itself as schismatic or even as anything essentially new. Rather, it sees itself as integral to the history of salvation and to the revelation of the Gospel everywhere and across time. It reads its own beginnings in the sixteenth century not as a series of new creations but as a reformation, as a renewed disclosure of the Gospel quite in harmony with all earlier disclosures. This is not to evade the problematic aspects of these histories, but it is to indicate that any historical difficulties must first submit to the confidence of Protestantism that they are internal to it and not external or extraneous (Bassett, 2001).

The Protestant doctrine of sola scriptura makes no idol of the Bible. This doctrine does not refer to the Bible essentially or as a material entity, as a physical presence, though it is impossible to think of the Bible apart from these things. Even here the reliability of Scripture is understood not to lie in its mere words. Protestantism has insisted that Scripture becomes binding for faith and practice through the internal witness of the Holy Spirit, internal to believer and that Church, that it is true and incumbent upon those who would be faithful (Bassett, 2001).

John Wesley does not specifically explain how he arrived at his theological conclusions, what his presuppositions were, which of them the authoritative sources were, what the truth-warrants were, or how the path to their declaration was chosen. Yet, the general lines of his theological reflection are sufficiently clear and coherent that they reveal an implicit theological method, a method that is, as it happens, completely in line with the Protestant Principle though Wesley probably never heard the term itself. Furthermore, while

Wesley's theological opinions were occasional in their application and often occasional in their conception as well, they were not off-hand. They were formed in consequence of a rigorous process. An annotated list of Wesley's controlling methodological principles must suffice here (Bassett, 2001).

What are the sources for authoritative theology and theologizing? Preeminence is given to Scripture, but it is Scripture as it is read and sung and practiced along the great and living history of the Church. All of these, including Scripture, acting in lively interplay, checking and balancing, are the source of authoritative theology and theological reflection. What is the relationship between theology and faith? Wesley believed theologically on the presupposition that while the theology works with revealed materials and with what is generated as the Holy Spirit brings the worshipping Church and those revealed materials into living contact, theology is not itself part of the revelation. Theology, for Wesley, is reflection upon the faith. It is not the faith itself. In this sense, theologizing is a subjective enterprise. Theology becomes objective, or authoritative, or canonical only as it may be assimilated into the tradition. Only as it becomes part of the living experience, the faith and practice, can the worshipping Church have its full impact. Having been so assimilated, theological reflection becomes faith (Bassett, 2001).

Wesley readily admits the humanity and time-bound character of the biblical documents. He insists that interpretation of them is a matter for faith. Scripture is to be reflected upon in faith. The humanity and the time-bound character of the Bible must not be submitted exclusively to the scrutiny that arises from a commitment to empirical reality alone. The Bible must be submitted to the scrutiny that arises from theological reflection as well (Bassett, 2001).

Wesley knew nothing of religious language as an academic theorist, but he did sense some language problems. On the one hand, he did not see the language of theology, or that of religion generally, as supernatural, as a matter of divine revelation. On the other hand, neither did he insist that meaning demand empirical referents, so that words such as "saved" or "God," for instance, must apply to some empirical reality or forfeit any claim to meaning. Ordinary words may carry religious meaning in religious contexts, meanings not attached to them in ordinary usage, without necessarily equivocating them semantically. "Perfection" is a significant example of this. It is more than a mere verbal symbol, and it is more than a mere vocal utterance with no clear empirical referent; existentially, it is less than what is now called an event; it is less than a word which, when evoked, changes the character of the situation in which it is evoked. So, "perfection" is used in a religious sense to describe a state that in some critical or essential sense cannot be improved upon, and thus relates to its usual non-religious usage. It is far removed from that usual non-religious usage insofar as the noun or pronoun to which it applies may not be perfect in the usual sense and may in fact be, from that usual perspective, the antithesis of perfection (Bassett, 2001).

The Holiness Movement is rich in resources and has much to offer the Church at large. Generally speaking, at least theologically, most of Protestantism has counted Holiness followers in. The Movement has tended to count Protestantism out in all but theory. The cost has been tremendous to Methodist teaching. Holiness inner history has made of it something that Methodists did not intend for it to become (Bassett, 2001).

Origin of the Holiness Movement

According to James M. Burkley, "Methodism did not originate in the Western hemisphere". "It was transported across the sea, planted in a fertile soil, and brought forth fruit after its own kind" (Burkley,

1898, pp. 1) The Western branch of the early church looked at sin and salvation the same way as the first judge. Sin is a legal problem, a judicial problem. A man is guilty, and the guilty person must be punished, unless there is someone else who is willing to be punished in place of the guilty one. We are all guilty and we owe God a big debt that we cannot pay. But Jesus paid it all; he took our place: he was punished for us. We are now set free; we are forgiven (Smith, 1962).

Perhaps one reason the Western Church with its center in Rome looked at sin and salvation in legal terms is because of the influence of Roman law. The Romans were known for their law. Perhaps the Roman Catholic Church patterned its understanding of sin, guilt, and absolution after the Roman legal system. When sin is committed, the sinner goes to confession and receives absolution. When another sin is committed, another trip to the priest is necessary for confession and absolution. The same thing is repeated over and over (Smith, 1962).

Protestantism, of course, rejected the Roman Catholic doctrine that we need priests to hear our confessions and to grant absolution. Instead, we can come to God directly and can confess our sins to Him. By faith, believers receive forgiveness or justification. God cancels the debt of sin because Christ took on himself the penalty for our sins. We may still be under the power of sin, but that does not matter because God no longer sees our sins. He sees us through the righteousness of Christ, and no longer considers us guilty. John Calvin and his followers developed this theology in its extreme form to the point where they could even say that we sin daily in word, thought and deed, but that does not mean the believer has lost his/her salvation. In fact, we can never lose our salvation because our salvation does not depend on us; it depends on God (Smith, 1962).

The Western Church believed that God created human beings perfect and complete. But then came the fall, when Adam and Eve used their freedom and disobeyed God. Adam and Eve became guilty before God. Human nature became sinful, and that sinful nature, or original sin, passed on to all human beings. All men and women have inherited the guilt of original sin. Human beings completely lost the image of God and their freedom to make any decisions. They were now free to do only one thing: commit the act of sin. Therefore, if there is going to be any salvation, it will have to come from God, and God alone (Smith, 1962).

The Eastern Church viewed sin as a disease in the human condition which needs healing. Forgiveness alone is not enough. If sin is a disease of human nature, then salvation is the healing of our sin-diseased nature. Sinners not only need pardon, but also power that would transform them inside and out. For example, habitual liars, adulterers, drug addicts, thieves, also middle class sins such as materialism, greed and workaholism need more than forgiveness. They need healing, transformation, cleansing, change of heart and mind (Smith, 1962).

The Western and Eastern branches of the early church also viewed the sacraments differently. The Western Church viewed baptism and the Eucharist (communion) as certification of justified status before God. When one is baptized, God has placed His seal of approval on that individual. Baptism takes away the guilt of original sin. That is why infants are baptized. Likewise, to receive the Eucharist one must first be properly certified. When one receives the Eucharist, the seal of approval remains in force. It was widely debated as to who may receive communion and who may not (Smith, 1962).

Likewise, there were debates as to who is qualified to bestow it or administer it and who is not. It means that the sacraments were viewed in legal or judicial terms. The Eastern Church viewed the sacraments differently. Baptism was a sacrament of cleansing and purification, not just the removal of guilt. Likewise, the Eucharist was viewed as the means by which the Holy Spirit continues to be present in us and continues the healing of our sin-diseased nature. Ignatius called it "the medicine of immortality." The question is not who is worthy, or who is not. No one is worthy. The sacrament is not a certification that we are okay. It is God's continued grace to bring healing and wholeness to us. Chrysostom taught that we are restored in the image of God by sharing in the nature of God. Such is the power of faith in Him, such the excess of His grace. And as the element of fire, when it meets with ore from the mine straightway of earth makes it gold, even so and much more Baptism makes those who are washed to be of gold instead of clay, the Spirit at that time falling like fire into our souls, burning up the "image of the earthy," and producing the "image of the heavenly," fresh coined, bright and glittering, as from the furnace mould (Smith, 1962).

In fact, to say it even more forcefully, the Eastern Church believed that God makes us more and more like Himself. God is continually restoring His image in us. We are in the process of becoming like God. The ultimate purpose is that our nature be like the nature of God, full of love, full of light (Smith, 1962).

The modern world challenges the old faith. On the eve of the American Civil War, the stream of Holiness preaching in the United States approached flood stage. A great revival swept the nation in 1858. Hundreds of mammoth daily prayer meetings broke out almost spontaneously in New York, Philadelphia, Chicago, and nearly every city and town in the northern states. Ministers and laymen of all denominations took part. Churches everywhere scheduled special services. A half-million people were converted. The deepening of moral conviction hardened resistance against the sin of slavery, soon to be done away in the Civil War, and rejuvenated as well the crusades against intemperance, Sabbath desecration, and neglect of the poor. It also inspired hundreds of Christians to seek Holiness of heart and life (Smith, 1962).

Just before and during the revival, pastors in Buffalo, Boston, and New York invited Charles G. Finney to conduct union services in those cities. Finney had had few such calls to the East since 1839, when he and Asa Mahan, together with other professors at Oberlin, a Congregationalist college in Ohio, had professed and begun to proclaim the grace of Entire Sanctification. Though never as clear or consistent in their teaching as Methodist theologians wanted them to be, Finney and Mahan thereafter preached Holiness all over the country (Smith, 1962).

One of their admirers, William E. Boardman, published in 1858 his book The Higher Christian Life. It soon made the author famous in both the United States and England; various publishers sold nearly 200,000 copies. Boardman attempted to make the southern experience more appealing to all denominations by describing it in terms which neither Methodist nor Oberlin preachers had used before. In New England, in the same year, A. B. Earle professed sanctification; for the next decade, he was the most influential Baptist evangelist. He ministered first at Fall River and New Bedford, Massachusetts, then at Tremont Temple, Boston. Earle launched the career of interdenominational soul winning in which he made the "Arrest of faith", as he called it, his most prominent doctrine (Smith, 1962).

Meanwhile, among the Methodists, the long campaign to restore the Wesleyan experience to its central place in that denomination proceeded with new earnest-ness. Phoebe Palmer, wife of a New York City physician, had for twenty years conducted worship services in her home. Normally a Tuesday Meeting for the Promotion of Holiness was organized. Hundreds of Methodist preachers, including at least two bishops and three individuals who would later hold that office, were sanctified under Mrs. Palmer's influence. The Guide to Holiness, printed in Boston, publicized her work and served as

THE HOLINESS EXPERIENCE AND ITS EVOLUTION

well to unite and inspire the clergymen great and small who shared her concern. Conflicts were brewing in some local sections of the church that in western New York produced the Free Methodist secession in 1859, but the Palmers and other Holiness evangelists were never in such demand at camp meetings and revivals as in the years just prior to the Civil War (Smith, 1962).

Many believed, in 1858, that the gospel of Christian Perfection was the key to a century of spiritual progress. Fifty years later, when the followers of Phineas F. Bresee, H. F. Reynolds, and C.B. Jernigan met in the tiny Texas town called Pilot Point to unite the fragments of the Holiness Movement, that doctrine had become an embattled creed. Bresee and Reynolds professed similar optimism, declaring that consolidation of the perfectionist forces would achieve that goal sooner. But sober men knew that the strongest argument for organized Holiness was the aggressive nature of its opposition. For a half-century thereafter the experience of sanctification thrived chiefly in small Wesleyan denominations. Only by the mid-twentieth century, when these groups numbered perhaps one million and a new atmosphere of spiritual hunger prevailed in the church world, could hopes arise for the restoration of the quest for perfect love to an important place in Protestant religion (Smith, 1962).

God had promised to pour out His Spirit on all flesh, in the last days. "Sons and daughters would prophesy and young men see visions" (Joel 2:28). It was not enough simply to cry that the stars were falling. Popular psychology, sometimes masquerading as Christians, prescribed confident thinking as the antidote to anxiety. By this, an individual was supposed to be able to redeem himself/herself from defeat and despair. Nazarenes at mid-century were convinced that the means to both personal and social health was the love of God shed abroad in men/women's hearts by the Holy Spirit. Thus the sixth decade of their history as a church found them intent upon discovering more effective ways to point the world to Christ and Holiness (Smith, 1962).

The breakout of Holiness revivals started in 1865. The Civil War left in its wake a moral and spiritual crisis that prominent Methodist pastors believed could be met only by a return to the faith of their founders. John C. McClintock, chairman of the committee in charge of the celebration of the denomination's one hundredth anniversary in 1866, declared that Christian Perfection was the central theme to the Bible and the chief goal of Wesleyan piety. McClintock the following year became the first president of Drew Theological Seminary, near New York City. He chose Randolph S. Foster, author of Christian Purity, the Heritage of Faith, to be professor of systematic theology (Smith, 1962).

During the centennial year, weekday Holiness meetings multiplied in many cities. Dr. and Mrs. Palmer enjoyed a highly successful tour of conference camp meetings in New York State, Michigan, and Illinois. They conducted revivals at several Methodist colleges, including one, which lasted three weeks at Garrett Biblical Institute, near Chicago. Frances Willard, future president of Woman's Christian Temperance Union, professed sanctification. In New York, meanwhile, John S. Inskip, chairman of the Methodist preachers meeting, led a series of discussions, which gave rise to the first national camp meeting for the promotion of Holiness. This gathering, held at Vineland, New Jersey, in 1867, bound together a rising group of young men who made a specialty of the Second Blessing. John Allen Wood, pastor at Wilkes-Barre, Pennsylvania, and William B. Osborn, a presiding elder in southern New Jersey, seem to have suggested the national camp. Other sponsors were Alfred Cookman, a distinguished Philadelphia minister; George Hughes, pastor at Trenton; Lewis R. Dunn, of Central Church Newark; and Bishop Matthew Simpson, the denomination's most illustrious preacher. So extensive were the fruits of the Vineland assembly that these men formed A National Camp Meeting Association for the Promotion of Holiness and planned a similar gathering each year (Smith, 1962).

A week later, four hundred persons, many of them ministers, professed to have received during this meeting the consciousness of sanctifying grace. Invitations for the next year's camp poured in from conference offcials all over the East and Midwest. Three were selected, each near an urban center of the church: Asbury Grove, a few miles north of Boston; Oakington, Maryland, on the railroad between Wilmington and Baltimore; and Des Plaines, Illinois, site of the Chicago District camp meeting (Smith, 1962).

Between national camp meeting engagements, members of the association promoted the Holiness revival in many other ways as well. As early as 1869, they launched a weekly paper, the Christian Standard and Home Journal. John Inskip was the first editor. The next year William McDonald founded in Boston a monthly magazine, The Advocate of Holiness. In 1873, an affiliate publishing company took over the Standard, under the presidency of Washington C. DePauw, Indiana glass manufacturer. Both presses issued a stream of books and pamphlets, swelling that which still poured in from the office of the Guide to Holiness. Dr. Palmer had purchased the latter in 1863, at which time he moved it to New York City and appointed his wife editor in chief (Smith, 1962).

The leaders of the movement also served as evangelists in hundreds of camp and revival meetings. At a camp meeting John Allen, sanctified at Vineland, became a revered figure in Maine. Dr. and Mrs. Palmer led the daily Holiness meetings there for many years. Alfred Cookman continued the annual round of Methodist camps in the Middle Atlantic States, as had been his custom since 1857. Shortly before his sudden death in the fall of 1871, Cookman preached before President U. S. Grant at Ocean Grove and before Massachusetts's notables at Martha's Vineyard. Bishop Simpson spoke at Cookman's funeral, and R. S. Foster, who had succeeded John McClintock as president of Drew Seminary, declared he was the most sacred man he had known (Smith, 1962).

John Inskip, meanwhile, resigned his Baltimore pastorate in the spring of 1871 in order to give all of his time to evangelistic labor. Bishop Edward R. Ames invited Inskip to accompany him that summer as a preacher to the St. Louis, Missouri, and Nebraska annual conference, an auspicious beginning to a brilliant ten years' work. When in 1881 William McDonald joined Inskip in a round-the-world mission, their annual conferences, the New York East and the New England, enthusiastically commended them to overseas Methodists, as did the presiding bishops, Thomas Bowman and Matthew Simpson. At Lucknow, India, they found their old friend William B. Osborn preaching earnest sermons on the baptism of the Holy Spirit and serving as presiding elder on the South India Conference, recently organized out of William Taylor's free-lance ministry at both Bombay and Lucknow (Smith, 1962).

Other champions of Holiness invested their time in educational, administrative, or literary work. Daniel Steele was elected the first president of Syracuse University in 1871, shortly after he professed sanctification. From there he went to Boston University as professor of New Testament Greek. From 1886 to 1891 he held the chair of systematic theology as well. He wrote many influential books on perfect love. Lewis R. Dunn published numerous articles in the church journals, in addition to several books. Asbury Lowery edited The Christian Standard after Inskip gave it up, and served thereafter as pastor and presiding elder. William Nast, the founder of German Methodism and an active member of the National Association, encouraged the drive to make Holiness the dominant theme of German-speaking churches and camp meetings (Smith, 1962).

The support of the bishops was from the outset a key factor in the spread of the Holiness revival. Edmund S. James, senior to Simpson and Ames, was a close friend and admirer of Mrs. Palmer. He wrote a glowing preface to the book of testimonies, which he published in 1872 Pronounced Friends of Holiness: Randolph S. Foster, Stephen M. Merrill, Jesse T. Peck, and Gilbert Haven. Peck, author of The Central Idea of Christianity, which the Methodist-publishing house reissued in 1875, had contributed often to the Guide of Holiness. Haven had the Zion Herald in Boston, and wrote the introduction to George Hughes history of the national camps (Smith, 1962).

Many such occurrences demonstrate how fully the leaders of the Holiness revival had overcome early fears that they might incite secessions from the church. The strength of their propaganda, in fact, lay in their constant appeals to the memory of Wesley, Fletcher, and the first American bishop, Francis Asbury. So successful were they in identifying sanctification with Methodist orthodoxy that opponents were hard pressed to find ground upon which to stand without laying themselves open to the charge of heresy. Later on, in the early 1890s, those who first published extensive criticisms of the doctrine had to acknowledge their divergence from Wesley's views. Only then, could opposition see, when the bright hope faded of sweeping the whole church into the pursuit of perfect love, did responsible champions of Holiness drift toward secession (Smith, 1962).

In focusing on the interdenominational and international aspects of the movement, what makes the story of the Holiness revival among men outside the Methodist church important is that they so often took the initial steps toward organizing new denominations. Among the Nazarene founding fathers, for example, William Howard Hoople was a Baptist, Edward F. Walker a Presbyterian,

J.O. McClurkan a Cumberland Presbyterian, and A.M. Hills and George Sharpe, of Scotland, Congregationalists. Most of these men had previously been active in interdenominational associations, which paid scant heed to the desires of Methodist officialdom. They were all heirs in some measure of either the Oberlin or Keswick movements, both of which had leaned toward congregational and independent church government (Smith, 1962).

After the Civil War, William E. Boardman and A.B. Earle found Presbyterians and Baptists everywhere willing to listen to the promise of the higher life. Earle conducted a long union revival campaign in Park Street Church, Boston, in 1866. He then went to California for two years, at the invitation of the San Francisco ministerial association. In the 1870's, A.P. Graves, one of Mrs. Palmer's converts, carried forward this Baptist phase of the work. In Boston, Charles C. Cullis, an evangelical Episcopal layman, opened a mission, a training school, a publishing business, and a rest home for sufferers from tuberculosis, all dedicated to propagating the higher life (Smith, 1962).

Meanwhile Boardman, Henry Belden, and Asa Mahan preached in camp meetings and revivals all over the East. Mahan expressed gratitude that the American Board of Commissioners for Foreign Missions had abandoned their former prejudice against candidates who espoused the Second Blessing. In 1873, when a national conference of Congregational churches met at Oberlin, its members asked the aged Finney to preach on the baptism of the Holy Spirit. The same year, Dwight L. Moody, who had for many months past enjoyed the higher life, opened the meetings in London, England, which made his name a household word on two continents (Smith, 1962).

The writings of Charles G. Finney, Phoebe Palmer, T.C. Upham, and William E. Boardman had circulated widely in England by the time of our Civil War, and Finney had made two memorable visits.

After the Awakening of 1858 spread overseas, Mrs. Palmer and her husband sailed on a four-year tour, which created a minor sensation in English Methodism (Smith, 1962).

The Palmers preached for weeks to packed houses at Leeds, Sheffield, Manchester, Birmingham, and dozens of other places. On their return, James Caughey, who had twice before conducted long campaigns in England, departed to carry on the crusade. Caughey stayed three and a half years and reported over 10,000 converts. Thereafter, British Methodists championed sanctification more unanimously than their American cousins in 1881. Both the General Committee of the Primitive Methodist church and prominent Wesleyan pastors welcomed their work. At Leeds, they saw scores of ministers profess the experience. Thirteen hundred persons were converted in one service (Smith, 1962).

Meanwhile, Dougan Clark and Asa Mahan carried the good news to English Friends and Congregationalists, and William E. Boardman helped inspire the large summer conferences, which bore permanent fruit in the famous Keswick Convention. Boardman and R. Pearsall Smith, a brilliant but erratic young Presbyterian minister, were thrown together in London during Dwight L. Moody's campaign of 1873. They joined in a small meeting for holiness at the London Y.M.C.A., in which Smith's wife, Hannah Whitall, daughter of a Philadelphia Quaker family, took a leading part. The following July, a wealthy squire held a convention on his estate and invited these two and about one hundred others, mostly clergyman and students from nearby Cambridge University. A similar conference held the same summer during vacation time at the sister university blossomed into An Oxford Union Meeting for the Promotion of Scriptural Holiness. Huge crowds flocked to the town. Asa Mahan was present and preached his first sermon. Though Boardman and Smith were not in charge, their personal influence was very great. At both meetings, influential preachers from Germany, France, and the Lowlands experienced the power of God (Smith, 1962).

The origin of the Holiness Movement was apparent. Many testimonies of the overpowering Spirit of God had been witnessed. At this point in church history the zeal to persuade and push the cause of the Holiness Movement to the forefront had arrived. The champions of the Holiness Movement would have the momentum to push the Holiness agenda to new levels.

Holiness and the African American Experience

The relationship of African Americans to the Holiness Movement cannot be overlooked. As early as 1887, the characteristics of African American worship in religious services had been noted. Given that the ultimate objective of worship in the Holiness church tradition is some form of spiritual manifestation, the aesthetic and ethical norms that govern movement toward this objective are derived from the Bible and black culture. The distinctive songs, speech, and dances of the Holiness church symbolically "usher" the saints "out" of this world and into a more authentic one discerned within sacred time and space. What makes this process exilic is the connection made between the saints' rejection of the world and the world's rejection of the saints (Sanders, 1996).

The believer rejects the world on the basis of biblically derived ascetic communications; that is, the mandate to Holiness. They are themselves "rejected" by the dominate host culture because of their race, and sometimes their sex and class. What is not so clear is whether there is consensus that the mandate to holiness dictates opposition to racism, sexism, and economic oppression. When the saints sing "Holy" unto the Lord, lift up holy hands, or do the dance, in effect, they are expressing their allegiance to a world in which God has determined who is accepted and who will receive power. Moreover, their worship shows that they believe God accepts the praise, performances, and aesthetic standards that are characteristic of Africans in diaspora (Sanders, 1996).

Holiness followers believe that they are freed from the pressure to conform to worship styles of the dominant culture. The believers are "in" a world that is sinful, oppressive, and discriminatory; they demonstrate that they are not "of" this world by purging themselves of its secularizing influences through rituals that meet their own criteria for cultural authenticity and biblical interpretation. In worship, the saints replicate the "other" world, the place where the exile can be at home. Ethically, their allegiance to this other world requires them to be loving, honest, and pure, even in relations with their enemies. Just as the sanctuary or temple is the place of spiritual experience their body is the temple of the Holy Spirit. Holy purity in the sanctuary requires purity of body, mind, and spirit outside of the sanctuary. By their worship, the saints manifest the holy character of the God they serve. By clean living, the saints demonstrate to the world that they possess the Spirit that possesses them in worship (Sanders, 1996).

In view of these various descriptions of worship in the Holiness church tradition and the suggestions made thus far with regard to how these data may be interpreted, it is now possible to identify some of the specific marks and symbols of worship where believers lose control of their bodies asking God to come and work through them. Such elements and events in worship that distinguish these churches from the white North American Protestant mainstream include the following list, which is hardly exhaustive: (1) dancing, (2) the "Yes" chant, (3) the use of white uniformed liturgical attendants, and (4) the inclusion of community announcements and the welcoming of visitors as liturgy. Many or most of these marks and symbols can be found in traditional liturgy. To characterize these facets of worship as "exilic" is to suggest that they are rooted in African culture and may be reflective of specific worship patterns and cultural practices associated with slave religion in the rural South (Sanders, 1996).

Shouting has been a norm for most African American congregations within the Holiness faith. The dance is best exemplified as the movement of the shout, the climactic expression of individual and collective spirit's impact that is especially characteristic of the Pentecostal congregations. In her article "Dancing to Rebalance the Universe: African American Secular Dance and Spirituality," Katrina Hazzard-Gordon commented that the dance serves as a "kinetic vocabulary" through which the needs, perceptions, impressions, and responses of African American people are articulated. Two of the distinct types of steps Hazzard-Gordon designates as "conduit steps" in the Holy Spirit's dealings are specifically related to the liturgical dancing of the sanctified church tradition: the "resting step," a simple shifting of the weight from side to side, from one foot to the other with a slight twisting away from the center of movement, as observed in the swaying motion of black gospel choirs; and the "shout step," a simple, two-footed rhythmic hopping up and down, often with the feet never leaving the floor. Her description of the juxtaposition of the "chaotic, the uncontrolled, and the unconscious" movements associated with the onset of God's power with the "ordered, contained, conscious, and controlled" conduit step is reflective of the static-ecstatic dialectic in sanctified worship (Sanders, 1996).

In this perspective, the concept of liturgical dance can be expanded to include choreographed choir processions and a whole host of bodily gestures by choir and congregation, such as swaying, patting of feet, clapping of hands, raising one or both hands, and spontaneous standing up. In the Holiness churches, there are saints who do not do the "shout step" associated with the Pentecostals but rather leap straight up and down when they "get happy." In addition, skilled liturgical dancers in some of the sanctified churches perform carefully choreographed and rehearsed dances to various types of sacred music. At the Third Street Church of God, the liturgical dance troupe, Praise in Motion, consists of young women who perform arranged dances to spirituals, gospel songs, and contemporary praise music. Although executed with great energy and enthusiasm, these liturgical dances are not ecstatic but would be more properly described as exemplary of the static form (Sanders, 1996).

Clearly, some church leaders within the Holiness churches have mastered the technique of inciting the holy dance through measured demonstration. Church leaders seem to have a definite sense of the aesthetic requirements of the ritual dance. Moreover, leaders attempted to convince others of the ethical propriety, even necessity, of ecstatic expression in worship. There were many African American Methodists who confirmed the notion of the shout as exilic liturgy. They argued that "shouting" was a conspicuous feature of early Methodism but was not restricted to the Methodists or particularly indigenous to the United States. Soon conflict resulted over the fact that the ring shout as a form of corporate praise with a lack of inhibition and restraint was not appropriate. Eventually, the shouters were "exiled" from the Methodists ranks because some Methodists were unhappy with the camp meeting type of worship. The constant efforts to restrain the shouters' exuberance included the rigid exclusion of the choruses and spiritual songs from the official Methodist hymnbook. The ring shout was preserved only among the "isolated hill people of southern Appalachia" and the blacks but otherwise a total lack of interest has been exhibited in the specific contributions African Americans made to the development of shouting in early American Methodism. The Old World origins of shouting are traced to the Irish and not the Africans (Sanders, 1996).

"British-American Methodist Traditions" provides a more balanced description of the influence of Africans and Europeans on the progressive ritualization of the shout and other dissociative experiences in American Protestant Christianity. Africans had a tremendous impact on ecstatic religious expression in American revivalism to the eighteenth century. Much of the Africanization of American Protestant religious dance took place under at least nominally Methodist auspices, the earliest account being that of John Watson, a Methodist preacher, who in 1819 observed dancing "very greatly like the Indian dances" in the "blacks' quarters" at the Philadelphia Annual Conference. Many observers related shouting to African culture and to the experience of slavery. The greater openness of traditional African culture to dissociative religious experience and the crisis of enslavement led African Americans to elaborate and institutionalize dissociative experience at the heart of their worship life in many ways that European Americans typically did not (Sanders, 1996).

Two generalizations contrasting African and European approaches to the sacred are (1) that music and movement are largely divorced in the European approach and integrally related in the African, and (2) that power is normally linked with equilibrium (balance, control) in the European context and with movement (transformation, change) in the African context. This suggests that Europeans may prefer static forms of spiritual empowerment, whereas Africans prefer ecstatic or dynamic forms (Sanders, 1996).

CHAPTER 3

DOCTRINAL SUES THAT CREATED NEW SCHOOLS OF THOUGHT

Many adherents of the Holiness Movement tend to say that its denominations formed as Methodism and others closed the doors to Holiness. However others feel that the facts regarding their separation were incomplete. The fact that many advocates of Entire Sanctification exited from the mainline bodies believing that those bodies would no longer tolerate their message has created yet another significant characteristic of the movement's inner history: the tendency to see itself as an outside critic of much of Protestantism. On the other hand, it has generally not been able to understand that criticism leveled at it by non-Holiness people is often offered as part of their own self-criticism. The inner history of Protestantism at large has counted the Holiness Movement in; the inner history of the movement has counted much of Protestantism out (Bassett, 2001).

Moving Beyond Methodism

Eventually, the Holiness Movement decisively parts company with Wesley. Wesley saw his work as a self-criticism of Protestantism, even of wider Christianity. He was very much the insider, seeking reform; not the outsider, forsaking the old to create the new. His theological method was designed to retain as much of the past as possible, as shown by his understanding of tradition, and to build and maintain theological ties with the various groups of his time. To be sure, he could and did sharply rebuke both his own Church of England and some independents. But this was as a responsible brother, not as a visiting inquisitor and certainly not as one who even could stand outside the circle of faith so long as it was clearly Christian by what he believed to be a proper definition. This is, of course, a consequence of Wesley's theological method and an expression of the Protestant Principle. It is never an end in itself, though he always feels he must answer to it for his message and method (Bassett, 2001).

For the most part, Wesley saw the Spirit as having worked, and working yet, even in groups that official Anglicanism condemned. There was no Christian ministry, until he and his co-laborers offered it; the success of the Gospel in cutting through a supposedly impervious socio-cultural condition gave footnotes to Wesley's growing belief that there may be faithlessness to insisting that the Gospel is dependent upon special forms and formulae (Bassett, 2001).

The fact that tradition, experience, and reason are sources of theological authority and reflection in dynamic conjunction with Scripture necessarily keeps religious thinking open to the creativity of the Spirit, and it implies that the Spirit is not limited to the here and now. But this does not open the door to relativism. The creative Spirit is the same Spirit who enlivens and gives witness to the truth of Scripture. And it is the specific task of Scripture, within the quadrilateral, to serve as the foundation for "norming" the other norms, by the inspiration of the Spirit (Bassett, 2001).

It would seem that the reaction of the Holiness Movement to the liberal reading of the Protestant Principle, a reading that finally did invite theological carelessness and untenable relativism into some quarters, moved it in a direction that would be unaffordable. It separated it from its mentor and, as is becoming evident, from precisely that theological method which would allow it to retain its purpose in full vigor across the multitude of cultures to which it feels called. The most obvious expression of that separation is the influence of Fundamentalism in the thinking of the movement. Another is the ethnocentrism that marks its doctrinal and ethical declarations (Bassett, 2001).

Entire Sanctification

No feature of Christianity is more strongly emphasized by those to whom its establishment in the world was committed than the breadth and depth of its ethical demands. The "salvation" which was promised in the "Gospel" or "Glad Tidings" which constituted its proclamation was just salvation from sin and unto holiness. In other words, it was a moral revolution of the most thoroughgoing and radical kind. "Sanctification" is the biblical word for this moral revolution, and in "sanctification" the very essence of salvation is made to consist of the believer's eternal security. According to I Thessalonians 4:3, "This is the will of God" for you, says the apostle to his readers in this very epistle, "even your sanctification." A great part of the epistle is given, accordingly, to commending the new converts for the progress they had already made in this sanctification and to urging them onward in the same pathway (Warfield, 1990).

No moral attainment is too great to be pressed on them as their duty, and moral duty is too minute to be demanded of them as essential to their Christian walk. The standard the apostle Paul has before him, and consistently applies to his readers, falls in nothing short of absolute perfection, a perfection which embraces in its all-inclusive sweep the infinitely little and the infinitely great alike. In the verses immediately preceding chapter four the apostle had been engaged in enumerating a number of details of conduct that he wished, especially, to emphasize to his readers. The word perfection does not necessarily mean the believer never sins but does not live to sin. An explanation is made of this instant in Paul's remarks found in Romans 7: 14-25. John speaks of this when he acknowledges the fact that believers sin and when they do sin they have an Advocate with the Father (I John 1:8-10, 2:1-2). Perfection should be understood in that believers do not live to sin but if they do sin forgiveness is available. God does not choose saints haphazardly, but instead chooses those believers who will embrace within their hearts the love of a heavenly Father who cares for them (Warfield, 1990).

It is important that believers understand perfect as a continual process of growing to the point of perfection (Phil. 3:12). The entirety, the completeness, the perfection of the sanctification of which it speaks is, in fact. the great burden of the passage. In contrast with the details with which the apostle had just been dealing, and which—just because they were details—could touch the periphery only of a perfect life, and that only at this or that point of the circumference, he here averts to the complete sanctification that does not merely touch but fills not only the periphery but the entire circle of the Christian Believer's life. It is a sanctification that is absolutely complete and that embraces the perfection of every member of the human fellowship, which the apostle here deals with (Warfield, 1990).

Observe the emphatic repetition of the idea of completeness. May the "God of Peace"—and this very designation of God, however, has its reference to the completeness of the sanctification, peace being the opposite of all division, distraction, and hesitation the apostle prays, "sanctify you completely, so as that ye may be perfect and wanting nothing that enters into the perfection of your hearts to the ends for which you were created" (James 1:4). And not content with this, he adds explanatorily, "And may your spirit and your soul and your body be preserved entire, perfect," and not that merely, but "blamelessly entire, perfect"; "blamelessly" here means a manner which is incapable of being accused of not coming up to its idea of completeness (I Thessalonians 5:23 King James Version) (Warfield, 1990).

The distribution of the personality to be perfected is divided into its component parts, and in turn, perfection is displayed in each. Not only are believers to be sanctified wholly, but every part (spirit, soul, and body itself) is to be kept blamelessly perfect. The apostle is not content, in other words, with the general, but he descends into the specific elements of the believer's being. And for each of these elements in turn he seeks a "blameless perfection," that the sum of them all, that we at large may be, indeed, "complete and entire, wanting nothing" (James 1:4) (Warfield, 1990).

Now, this enumeration of parts is, in a sense, rhetorical and not scientific. The apostle is accumulating terms to convey the great idea of completeness more pungently to believers somewhat as Jesus did when He said, "we must love the Lord our God with all our heart and soul and mind and strength" (Matt. 22:37). But even so he makes a certain distinction among the three elements he enumerates, by the accumulation of which he expresses completeness most emphatically. His meaning is that there is no department of man's being into which he would not have this perfection penetrate, where he would not have it reign, and through which he would not have it operate to the perfecting of the whole (Warfield, 1990).

By this double mode of accumulation, the apostle throws an astonishing emphasis on the perfection for his readers. Certainly no doctrine of "Entire Sanctification" has been invented in current times that can compare with Paul's doctrine in height or depth or length or breadth. The perfection proposed is a real perfection (which is not always true of recent teachings on this subject), and the man who attains it is a perfect man- every part of his being receiving its appropriate perfection (which is seldom or never true of recent teachings) (Warfield, 1990).

Paul does not speak of this perfecting of the entire man as if it were a mere ideal, unattainable, and to be looked up to only as the forever beckoning standard hanging hopelessly above believers. He treats it as distinctly attainable. He seriously desired that believers would press for the prize, (Phil. 3:10-15) (Warfield, 1990).

He does not, indeed, represent it as attainable by and through human effort alone, as if man in his own strength could reach and touch this true ultimate goal of endeavor. Rather, he emphatically represents it as the gift of God alone (Phil. 4:13). After exhorting men to their best endeavors, he turns suddenly from man to God and besieges Him with prayer. He says, "Strive always, do this thing and do that and so work out this, your ethical salvation". The whole gist of Paul's prayer—the whole drift of his discourse—would be stultified, were it not so. Paul's prayer, and the way in which he introduces his prayer, all combine to make it certain that he is not mocking Saints here with an illusory hope but is placing soberly before believers an attainable goal. This perfection is then, necessarily, according to Paul, attainable for man. God can and will give it to His children (Warfield, 1990).

Paul prays seriously for this perfection for his readers, which implies that it may not be given to them; he definitely promises it to them, and bases this, his definite promise, on a foundation no less firm than the faithfulness of God. Thus Paul pledges the faithfulness of God to the completion of his readers' perfection. The believer must not lose the force and focus with which he does this by failing to pay attention to the sharp, proverbial character of this pledging clause. It has all the quality of a maxim and the gist of the maxim is that God, this God to whom Paul was praying for our perfection, is a hearer and doer. He has called believers into the Christian life, which is in principle a life of moral perfection. He is not only a God that hears but He is a God that also accomplishes. His very calling us into this life of new morality is a pledge, then, that He will perfect the good work in believers which He has begun. According to I Thessalonians 5:24, Paul writes, "Faithful is He that calleth you, who also will do it." (Warfield, 1990)

The accomplishment of Christian Perfection does not hang on weak endeavors. It does not hang even on Paul's strong prayer. It hangs only on God's almighty and unfailing faithfulness. And assuredly it goes in this, far, far beyond all modern teaching as to Entire Sanctification that ever has been heard of among men. It is a new dispensation that the apostle Paul assigns the accomplishment of this great hope (Warfield, 1990).

It is at once evident that Paul is not dealing with this perfection as a thing already in the possession of his readers. Paul thanks God, indeed, for their rescue from the state in which they were by nature. He thanks God for their great attainments in Christian living. A great part of the letter is taken up with exhortation to Christian duties not yet overtaken, graces of Christian living still to be cultivated. Not in and of them, but in and of God, is the perfection prayed for. Things that are seen by believers are not hoped for, and what believers pray for is not already attained. Moreover the very pledge he gives of the attainment of this perfection bears in it an implication that it is yet a matter of hope, not of possession. He pledges the faithfulness of God, the Caller. Accordingly, the perfection longed for and promised is not given in the call itself; it is not the invariable possession of the Christian soul (Warfield, 1990).

It is clear, therefore, that Paul, though promising this perfection as the certain heritage of every Christian man, presents it as a matter of hope, not yet seen, not as a matter of experience, already enjoyed. Believers can learn from Paul what believers can hope for. Assuredly, he has not left believers in ignorance here. He openly declares, indeed, the term of our imperfection—the point of entrance into our perfection. "May the God of peace," he prays, "sanctify you wholly and may there be preserved blamelessly perfect your spirit and soul and body, at the coming of our Lord Jesus Christ" (I Thes. 5:23). It is on the second advent of Christ, the end of the world, that the apostle has his eyes set. That is the point of time to which he refers the completeness of our perfecting (Warfield, 1990).

It is the perfecting of the whole person that he prays for, and this expressly includes the body as well as the soul and spirit. Now the perfected body is given to man only at the resurrection, at the last day, which is the day of the second coming of Christ. Until then the body is moldering in the grave. Whether spiritual perfection may be attained before then, he does not say in this passage. But the analogy of the body will apparently go so far as this, at all events: it raises a suspicion that the perfecting of the soul and spirit also will be gradual, the result of a process, and will be completed only in a crisis, a cataclysmic moment, when the Spirit of God produces in them the fitness to live with God. This suspicion is entirely borne out by Paul's dealing with the whole matter of sanctification in this context, and in this whole epistle, as a matter of effort, long continued and strenuous, building up slowly the structure to the end (Warfield, 1990).

Conflicting Views Regarding Holiness Teaching

Another way to make observations regarding Holiness teaching is to say that the movement developed an essentially defensive inner history, which it did not need to do. In fact, its own resources in systematic and constructive theology, those which present the doctrine of Entire Sanctification in its full theological context, in contrast to much of the specialized material on that doctrine in isolation, have generally aligned themselves with the inner history of Protestantism at large and have submitted to the Protestant Principle without the slightest betrayal of the Movement's signal tenet. But more important, it is precisely the doctrine and experience of Entire Sanctification, which calls believers to positive alignment with the inner history of Protestantism at large and calls believers to retain the Protestant Principle. Further, without that alignment and without that retention (in some quarters of the Holiness Movement it would be a restoration), the doctrine itself is threatened with criticism but it cannot overcome the personal testimonies of the Holiness following (Bassett, 2001).

The inner history of Protestantism has focused special interest on the doctrines of sola gratia, sola scriptura, and the universal priesthood of believers. A unique relationship exists between each of these and the doctrine of Entire Sanctification. In each case, the latter doctrine provides a rich and fruitful "soil" for explication and development. On the other hand, remove serious, fundamental attention to these three doctrinal "boundaries" and the doctrine of Entire Sanctification becomes an absurdity (Bassett, 2001).

Consider the case of the relationship of sola gratia to Entire Sanctification. The doctrine sola gratia/sola fide is the expression of the creative sovereignty of God from the perspective of soteriology.' It denies ultimate saving efficacy to any human religious activity. This much, Protestantism at large has seen clearly. But the dimension that the Wesleyan doctrine of Entire Sanctification brings to this doctrine is much grander. First of all, the Wesleyan understanding can take very seriously the positive side of the Protestant Principle that much of historic Protestantism has neglected in its proclamation of sola gratia/sola fide. The positive side asserts that the power of the Gospel is such that it can manifest itself in any human situation. The doctrine of Entire Sanctification is a grand declaration that the fullness of God's love is available to all, here and now, in any "here and now." Further, in anchoring itself in perfect love rather than in perfect behavior, the doctrine of Entire Sanctification is a declaration of the power of the Gospel to be expressed as Gospel across cultures (Bassett. 2001).

The principle tenet of the Movement also adds a dimension to the negative side of the Protestant Principle as it applies to sola gratia/sola fide. It stoutly affirms that just as ultimate saving efficacy must be denied to any human activity, it must not be denied to God Himself in the human life that has turned itself to Him. It declares that the creative sovereignty of God can make a truly new creature in Christ Jesus, even here (Bassett, 2001).

Such an enrichment of the understanding of sola gratia/sola fide is very much within the range of the Movement's present resources. On the other side of the matter, without this great Protestant declaration, the doctrine of Entire Sanctification is totally eviscerated. The utter inability of the human being to love God and neighbor is patent. The doctrine of Entire Sanctification must root itself in grace (Bassett, 2001).

The doctrine of sola scriptura expresses the negative side of the Protestant Principle by denying to any merely human word or idea superiority to the Word of God. And lest there is a temptation to mistake the fact that the Bible is in human language for mere humanity for the book itself, sola scriptura has included the insistence on the testimonium Spiritus sancti. Sola scriptura expresses the positive side of the Protestant Principle as the vehicle of ordinary language, enlivened and attested by the Spirit, becoming a means of grace. The Wesleyan doctrine of Entire Sanctification supports and enriches this doctrine by its declaration that the Word of God is to be taken with utter seriousness, even at that point where it would seem to speak only of a spiritual ideal for the believer and for society. That word of perfect love is not to be contravened by any human word, no matter how wise (Bassett, 2001).

Here, the corollary of the testimonium spiritus sanctus is of special importance. On the one hand, it means that the Word is carried to the believer in a way tailored to that given believer, and it is carried to a society in a way tailored to that society. And as it is the Spirit Himself Itself bearing the witness, so it is the Spirit who enables obedience. Thus, believers are again at the heart of the doctrine of Entire Sanctification (Bassett, 2001).

Without giving serious and basic attention to the doctrine of sola scriptura, with its corollary, the doctrine of Entire Sanctification lapses into a series of ethical or psychological platitudes absolutely untenable. This is, of course, a clear and present danger; especially as so much Holiness preaching is done in ignorance of the Scripture and depends instead upon analogies from interpretation of the eisegesis of a Biblical passage without regard for its original intention or context. That is to say, preaching is done without regard for the authentic testimonium Spiritus sancti, which involves tradition, experience, and reason (Bassett, 2001.

The doctrine of the universal priesthood of believers expresses the negative side of the Protestant Principle by denying to any human being or to any group of persons saving efficacy or intimacy. It declares all believers to be mediators, not owners or generators, of the creative sovereignty of God. On its positive side, the Protestant Principle is seen in the very universality of the priesthood. Again, here is the declaration that the Gospel can penetrate anywhere and manifest itself there. Priesthood is a concomitant of belief, not of status, office, culture or human nomination (Bassett, 2001).

Entire Sanctification enriches this doctrine on the negative side by insisting that perfect love is perfect submission, a submission that has everything to do with agapeic service to one's neighbor and the wholehearted devotion of the community of believers to the same service to society. On the positive side, the doctrine of Entire Sanctification affirms the willingness of the Spirit to enter in fullness any believer anywhere. That believer, already mediating his/her own culture, then becomes a mediator of the reconciling will of God in that culture (Bassett, 2001).

Without the doctrine of the universal priesthood of believers continually and profoundly pressed, the doctrine of Entire Sanctification destroys itself in self-righteousness and pride. Here it is that the self-critical temper is most necessary but also most likely, theologically. If the believer is truly a mediator of grace, of Gospel, and if the society of believers is a society of mediators, in the Spirit, there should develop a grand and positive enterprise of loving correction and encouragement, of reminding that believers do not own the vineyard but are its tenants. Agapeic service in perfect obedience is the mode of the priest, not self-preservation (Bassett, 2001).

The Gift of the Holy Spirit

The Scriptures are very clear about the fact that the Holy Spirit does give sifts to individual persons so that the whole body (the church) can be edified and can perform her function in any given age (Ephesians 4:7-12).

Revival in the church, however, like progress in any area of life, can also be fraught with dangers. As many believers began to experience the power and benefits of the Holy Spirit, disputes and indifference escalated among followers of the religious cause. It is important that all believers follow after the truth found in God's word. According to the Bible, "For as many as are led by the Spirit of God, they are the sons of God" (Romans 8:14). In discovering the truth, there is danger of failing to see this truth in the context of other truths just as important to the total plan of God. The inspiration and joy of it can so enthrall believers that they lose sight of everything else, and begin to ride it as a hobby. The only way to be guided through new experiences and to have waves of truth breaking through to believers is to test these by the Bible. It is important to encourage believers to look at several basic facts taught in the Bible about the gifts of the Spirit to the church (Rice, 1975).

The "Gift of the Spirit" and the "Gifts of the Spirit" are two distinct dimensions of the work of the Holy Spirit to the believer. Peter addressed many believers on the Day of Pentecost who asked, "Men and brethren, what shall we do?" His answer was, "Repent and be baptized every one of you in the name of Jesus Christ for the remission of sins, and ye shall receive the gift of the Holy Ghost" (Acts 2:38). Several messages seem to come through from these words of Peter. He is not referring to any gift such as teaching, preaching, healing, prophecy, tongues, or discernment. He is simply stating that the Gift that is to be received is the Holy Ghost Himself.

Furthermore, these must have been new converts in coming to know Jesus Christ as Lord and Savior. This was not a subsequent experience, because all the basic elements of a first-time commitment were repentance and baptism in the name of Jesus Christ.

This is the route for all believers becoming Christians. One of the problems of confusion about the work of the Holy Spirit is that the believer has a tendency to identity oneself with some subsequent work of grace after one is saved. But the simple truth is that the new birth involves receiving the Holy Spirit (1 Peter 1:4).

God promises that believers become partakers in the divine nature. Divine nature simply means the very nature of God. The Holy Spirit brings that new life. Having received the Holy Spirit and being born into God's family, a very simple question needs to be answered. What is the purpose of God's wanting to indwell His children by His Spirit? Some people believe the purpose is just to make the individual feel good. Others think they are saved just to go to Heaven, but that is not the primary reason because that will come when life is ended (Rice, 1975).

The only answer that fits the Bible teaching is that believers are saved to serve here and now. Isaiah 43:7 implies that believers are created for God's honor and glory. To put it very simply, individuals were created to fulfill the purpose and plan of God now. This is the believer's day to live for Him. Salvation is God's way of bringing Christians into the kind of relationship with Him where they can fulfill the plan He has for mankind (Rice, 1975).

To perform service for the Lord requires that one be qualified and empowered. It is precisely for this reason that the Holy Spirit gives "gifts." The Scripture passages which name the gifts are Romans 12:4-8, 1 Corinthians 12:7-11, and Ephesians 4:7-13. From these verses basic truths can be established regarding spiritual gifts (Rice, 1975).

Dangers lurk along the pathway of any Christian believer who is conscious that God has given him/her a special gift by the Holy Spirit. First of all, there is the danger of using the gift for personal gain and prestige.

There are believers who proudly say God has given me this unique gift, and I am the only one for miles around who has it. Some get caught in the net of "a good feeling." As with other dimensions of our Christian life, there is the possibility of some trying to exercise their gifts entirely apart from the larger body. They develop a "go it alone" strategy and set out to build their own little kingdom apart from the church. All believers must guard against these dangers. Paul mentions three positive purposes for the giving of gifts to individual believers in Ephesians 4:12. First, believers are given gifts "for the perfecting of the saints." The perfecting of the saints means the maturing of the believers. God wants His followers to grow up and be strong in the Lord and in the power of His might. When something is perfected, the wrinkles are ironed out; the lamp is trimmed and cleaned so that believers can better accomplish our purpose in the kingdom of God (Rice, 1975).

Secondly, Paul says the gifts are given "for the work of the ministry" (Eph. 4:12). The word "ministry" here is taken by some to mean the work of the preacher or pastor, but this is not the primary meaning of the word. Ministry simply means the work which the church is called to do for her Lord." As Christians, believers have a ministry to perform for Christ. Christian believers are commanded by our Lord to preach the Gospel to every nation, to then baptize the believers, and to teach again all those things that pertain to Christian living. Spiritual gifts given among individual believers are for the purpose of fulfilling this command (Rice, 1975).

Paul also says that gifts are given "for the edifying of the body of Christ" (Eph. 4:12). The word "edifying" comes from a word meaning "to build up morally; to make strong." Christ wants his church to be an example of good in a world that has become angry with sin, rebellion, and blindness. Jesus said, "The church we would be a light to the world" (Matt. 5: 14), but it takes power to shine out in a dark world. So the various gifts of the Spirit are given to the church to help her be a true representative of her Lord in any age, regardless of how dark the world may become (Rice, 1975).

The church must not only make allowance for the exercise of the various gifts of the Spirit to the believers, but she must also give guidance at this very point to keep individuals from splintering off into separate groups. The Holy Spirit not only speaks to the individual believer, but also to the body, the community of believers. This makes a good check and balance system to keep things on the level. That individual person who believes God is calling him/her to do a certain task through a gift he/she has received is wise in having other believers pray with him/her about it. In Acts 15:28, at the Jerusalem Annual Conference of the early church, God spoke to the church, saying, "For it seemed good to the Holy Ghost and to us." The individual must recognize the Holy Spirit's word of the church, and the church must also recognize the word of the Holy Ghost to the individual. The two need not be in conflict as much as believers are prone to think at times, but do very often give Christian followers the opportunity to test the spirits whether they be of God or not (I John 4:1-3).

CHAPTER 4

PENTECOSTALISM: IN OFFSHOOT OF THE HOLINESS MOVEMENT

The history of the Holy Spirit's dealings with human beings goes back to the very beginning of the human race. The history of the Holy Spirit's dealings with the church is about 2000 years long. The Spirit has been there all along, not when there are "manifestations" but when love was made manifest between people, when God's word was spread and God's will was sought, and when ordinary Christians ate bread of righteousness and called forth the wonders of a godly life. People have been baptized, inspired, healed, comforted, taught, led, and empowered. This was all made possible by the work of the Holy Spirit in the church (Longman, 2001b).

Making the claim that the Spirit's history in the modern church started at Azusa Street experience is in error. Pentecostalism had a history before Azusa, just as all human beings have history in their mother's womb. And those who have been taught about Azusa are as often as not taught a whitewashed version of what happened. Other streams of thought and practice, especially in the black and Anabaptist churches, also played a role in shaping Pentecostalism, but those streams were either not written down or were passed along in a very doubtful form, and thus are now lost to believers (Longman, 2001b).

In 1400 A.D. Vincent Ferrer, an itinerant Dominican preacher (1351-1419), preached in the western Mediterranean area. His speaking, and the results of it, bore a strange resemblance to modern Pentecostalism. He sometimes preached about the end times, apparently even claiming that the Antichrist was alive in his time. Reports were made of healings, and of many manifestations, including shaking and possibly glossolalia. The downside of Ferrer's work was that he persecuted and tortured Jews in order to put fear into them and force conversions (Longman, 2001b).

In the late 18th century, the Wesleys led a reform movement within the Church of England that eventually became Methodism. In 1790, Manuel De Lacunza (under the pen name "Ben-Ezra") wrote The Coming of the Messiah in Glory and Majesty: The book spoke prophetically of the events of Daniel and Revelation as actually taking place in history that had not come to pass. The book was "indexed" (banned) by the Catholic Church by 1824, but Edward Irving had the book translated and published in England conveying end-times views (Longman, 2001b).

In August of 1801, strange stirrings occurred in Kentucky, where a few dozen people would gather to hear preachers talk in exciting ways not unlike those of Jonathan Edwards in the Great Awakening. Only, it was a bit folks and a bit more emotional. Barton Stone studied what was happening and wanted to see if it would work on a larger scale, so he set up a "sacramental meeting" around his Cane Ridge Presbyterian meeting house, not far from Lexington,

Kentucky. It was planned to be the largest preaching event the area had yet seen, but no one was prepared for how big it was going to be. The preachers came from many denominations, but they had common threads in their message: they called on everyone to put their sins behind them, commit themselves to Christ, and live a holy life. The crowds reacted with vigor by fainting, shaking, jerking, and singing. At its peak, 20,000 appeared at the scene; by the time it was done, about 40,000 had been there at some time. Many, perhaps most of them, were not churchgoers. What was to be a weekend meeting became a week-long event of almost non-stop preaching even in the early hours of the day following. Cane Ridge set the stage for the "camp meeting" revivalism which swept the United States for the rest of the century (Longman, 2001b).

The camp meeting revivals were the scene that birthed revivalist Methodist and Baptist churches, and eventually led to Finney-style Congregationalism, the Holiness Movement, Pentecostalism, and the modern Evangelical movement (Longman, 2001b).

In 1825, Johann Adam Moehler, a German Catholic, published his book Unity in the Church. Moehler held that the Church is a living organic community (a body) put together and given gifts by the Holy Spirit. His most lasting contribution was his influence on Catholic thought regarding the Church as the Mystical Body of Christ.

In 1843, Johann Blumhardt began praying for a dying girl, placed his hands on her, and she was healed. The miracle drew people from all over Western Europe, although Blumhardt himself insisted that it was not his hands that healed, but God's response to honest prayer. Blumhardt saw sickness as a way that the Devil's power was brought to bear on our sin-soaked lives. He believed that the way to resist sickness is to confess our sin and change our ways. As years went by, he stressed searching the soul to find "hidden sins" that could be making believers ill. However, he did not believe that one could become perfect or sin-free before God in this lifetime, which to him was why all believers become ill (Longman, 2001b).

In 1845, John Morgan, of Charles Finney's Oberlin College, wrote in the Oberlin Quarterly (issue 1, p. 115) that "the baptism of the Holy Ghost, then, in its Pentecostal fullness, was not to be confined to the Primitive Church, but is the common privilege of all believers." Finney's own view of "the baptism of the Holy Spirit" was not much different from most evangelists of his day.

Yet, Morgan and others from Oberlin College, especially Henry Cowles, and from the Finney revivals were rethinking what that baptism meant, in light of the Finney revivals' vigorous manifestations (Longman, 2001b).

In 1851, the power of God used Dorothea Trudel to heal several colleagues in Mannedorf, Switzerland, by way of prayer and anointment with oil. She went on to found several faith-healing centers, or "faith homes," using the same methods plus close attention to living a Christian way of life. Her main associate was Samuel Zeller (Longman, 2001b).

In 1856, William Arthur published The Tongue of Fire, a Holiness book that signaled the start of a shift among some Holiness people in a direction that would lead to Pentecostalism. His prayer at the end of the book asks God to send the greatest demonstration of the Spirit's power ever (Longman, 2001b).

In 1862, Charles Cullis came to a Phoebe Palmer "Tuesday Meeting" in New York in major personal distress, and came to the faith there. Cullis became determined to take the Gospel (and the Holiness message on perfection) to the poor and ill. He founded orphanages, schools, and health institutions. In 1869, after reading about Dorothea Trudel's work, faith healing became a full part of his approach. Cullis worked hard to lead Holiness leaders to accept this merging of the two streams. He did this so well that later, when Holiness gave birth to Pentecostalism and Pentecostalism gave birth to the Charismatic Movement, faith healing was seen as a natural part of the new developments. Cullis's gospel events in the rest of the 19th Century created a platform for his combination of Holiness doctrine and faith healing, and the general public and press looked on with wonder and puzzlement (Longman, 2001b).

In 1871, while Chicago burned, Dwight Moody was burning, too, with a very different flame. His successful church was burned in the great fire, but right at that time he underwent a shakedown experience from praying with two of his female parishioners who said that he was lacking the power of the Spirit. He went on to be a major U.S. revivalist preacher. He emphasized many of the same things Holiness and Pentecostal believers did, but in a different way (Longman, 2001b).

In the 1870s, Elena Guerra (1835-1914), a Catholic educator of young women, popularized a discipline practice called the New Cenacle. In it, the ten days between Ascension and Pentecost are spent in prayer, meditation and devotion, to prepare for the coming of the gifts of the Holy Spirit on Pentecost, just as Christ's followers did in their upper room after He ascended. She had a broad view of what those gifts were, and held that the Spirit had great gifts for the common believers of her day. She even received the attention and support of Pope Leo XIII for her activities. She believed very strongly that the Church was paying far too little attention to the Spirit. Her work made for a greater public awareness of the Holy Spirit, especially among those who were likely to emigrate to the U.S. (Long-man, 2001b).

Also somewhere in this time, most likely the early 1870's, was William Doughty's ministry in New England, which may have included some form of speaking in tongues and certainly shaking, fainting, and dancing. His following would later unite with what was developing in the South (Longman, 2001b).

A key figure for the Holiness movement among African-Americans at this time was Amanda Berry Smith (1837-1915). She preached in the U.S., England, and Africa spreading a Palmer-flavored Methodism. She also wrote an autobiography.

Holiness had come to accept the theology of a "Second Blessing" separate from salvation and water baptism, and Methodism had come to reject it. In the largest split, tens of thousands left the Methodist Church to form the Church of the Nazarene. The most telling name for one of these Holiness splinters from Methodism was that of Ambrose Crumpler's Pentecostal Holiness Church.

In 1895, Benjamin Irwin, a former lawyer and Baptist convert to Holiness theology, had an experience of the "baptism of fire," He then formed the Fire-Baptized Holiness Church. From that experience, he fashioned a system of spiritual baptisms, each of which he gave names (such as "lyddite"). He also created the idea of a "third blessing" after separate blessings of salvation and sanctification. His life spun out of control from that time on, and in 1900 Irwin had to publicly confess his sins and step aside from church leadership (Longman, 2001b).

In December of 1900, traveling Holiness preacher Charles Parham was having a year-end series of revival meetings in Topeka, Kansas, when one of the women there, Methodist Agnes Ozman, spoke in existing languages she did not know. The effect on those present was, to understate the case, overpowering. From then on, a steady stream of tongues-speaking flowed from Parham's work. Parham and his students began to teach others about speaking in tongues. In Parham's travels, he met man of the popular and radical Holiness preachers, such as Alexander Dowie, a faith healer from the Chicago area, and Ben Irwin. These gifted preachers caused him to be overwhelmed, with few exceptions, they committed the sins they most preached against, and did them in a wanton and cynical way (Longman, 2001b).

In 1905, one of Parham's students, Lucy Farrow, provided the means for Parham to teach some courses in Houston, Texas. One of the students she sent to him was William Seymour, a black who was apparently about to become a minister in the Church of God (Anderson, IN). According to the segregation law and the landlord, and enforced by Parham, Seymour had to sit in the hallway instead of the classroom because he was black. However, Seymour must have learned his lessons well, since he would soon organize a ministry whose effects are being felt all over the world. He was one of the pioneers that blazed the trail to begin one of the largest religious movements in the world. Meanwhile, Farrow was the first key networker and "prayer warrior" of the Pentecostal Movement, giving her help wherever help was needed (Longman, 2001b).

Pre-pentecostal History

Since Pentecostalism began primarily among American Holiness believers, it would be difficult to understand the movement. Indeed, for the first decade practically all Pentecostals, both in America and around the world, had been active in Holiness churches or camp meetings. Most of them were Methodists, former Methodists, or people from kindred movements that had adopted the Methodist view of the Second Blessing. They were overwhelmingly Arminian in their basic theology and were strongly perfectionist in their spirituality and lifestyle (Synan, 2001).

In the years immediately preceding 1900, American Methodism experienced a major Holiness revival in a crusade that originated in New York, New Jersey, and Pennsylvania following the Civil War.

Begun in Vineland, N.J, in 1867 as the National Holiness Camp Meeting Association, the Holiness Movement drew large crowds to its camp meetings, with some services attracting over 20,000 people. Thousands claimed to receive the Second Blessing of sanctification in these meetings. Leaders in this movement were Methodists such as Phoebe Palmer (also a leading advocate of women's rights to minister); John Inskip, a pastor from New York City; and Alfred Cookman, a pastor from New Jersey (Synan, 2001).

From 1867 to 1880, the Holiness Movement gained increasing force within the Methodist churches as well as in other denominations. During this period, many Holiness advocates felt that this movement might revive the churches and bring new life to Christianity worldwide. After 1875, the American Holiness Movement, influenced by the Keswick emphasis, began to stress the Pentecostal aspects of the Second Blessing, some calling the experience "Pentecostal Sanctification." An entire hymnody was produced which focused on the upper room and a revolutionary "old-time Pentecostal power" for those who spent time praying at the altar. The songs celebrated the Second Blessing as both a cleansing and an endowment of power (Synan, 2001.

The Holiness Movement enjoyed the support of the churches until about 1880 when developments disturbing to ecclesiastical leaders began to emerge. Among these was a "come-outer" movement led by radicals who abandoned any prospects of renewing the existing churches. Led by such men as John B. Brooks, author of The Divine Church, and Daniel Warner, founder of the "Evening Light" Church of God in Anderson, Indiana, this movement spelled the beginning of the end of the dream of remaking the churches in a Holiness image. At the same time, other radicals began promoting such new teachings as "sinless perfection." a strict dress code of outward Holiness, marital purity, and a "third blessing" baptism of fire after the experience of sanctification (Synan, 2001).

The History of Pentecostalism

The first "Pentecostals" in the modern sense appeared on the scene in 1901 in the city of Topeka, Kansas in a Bible school conducted by Charles Fox Parham, a Holiness teacher and former Methodist pastor. In spite of controversy over the origins and timing of Parham's emphasis on glossolalia, all historians agree that the movement began during the first days of 1901 just as the world entered the Twentieth Century.

It was not until 1906, however, that Pentecostalism achieved worldwide attention through the Azusa Street revival in Los Angeles led by the African-American preacher William Joseph Seymour. He learned about the tongues-attested baptism in a Bible School that Parham conducted in Houston, Texas in 1905." He was invited to pastor a black Holiness church in Los Angeles in 1906. Seymour opened the historic meeting in April of 1906 in a former African Methodist Episcopal (AME) church building at 312 Azusa Street in downtown Los Angeles (Brown, 1997).

What happened at Azusa Street has fascinated church historians for decades and has yet to be fully understood and explained. For over three years, the Azusa Street "Apostolic Faith Mission" conducted three services a day, seven days a week, where thousands of seekers received the tongues baptism. Word of the revival was spread abroad through The Apostolic Faith, a paper that Seymour sent free of charge to some 50.000 subscribers. From Azusa Street, Pentecostalism spread rapidly around the world and began its advance toward becoming a major force in Christendom (Synan, 2001).

The Azusa Street Movement seems to have been a merger of white American Holiness religion with worship styles derived from the African-American Christian tradition which had developed since the days of slavery in the South. The expressive worship and praise at Azusa Street, which included shouting and dancing, had been common among Appalachian whites as well as southern blacks. The mixture of tongues and other teachings with black music and worship styles created a new and indigenous form of Pentecostalism that was to prove extremely attractive to disinherited and deprived people, both in America and other nations of the world (Synan, 2001).

The interracial aspects of the movement in Los Angeles were a striking exception to the racism and segregation of the times. The phenomenon of blacks and whites worshipping together under a black pastor seemed incredible to many observers. Frank Bartleman, a white Azusa participant described it best when he said, "The color line was washed away in the blood." Indeed, people from all the ethnic minorities of Los Angeles, a city that Bartleman called "the American Jerusalem, were represented at Azusa Street (Synan, 2001).

The Pentecostal Holiness Church

The first Pentecostal churches in the world were produced by the Holiness Movement prior to 1901. After becoming Pentecostal, members of the Pentecostal church retained most of the Holiness perfectionist teachings. Such teachings included the predominantly African-American Church of God in Christ (1897), the Pentecostal Holiness Church (1898), the Church of God with headquarters in Cleveland, Tennessee (1906), and other smaller groups. These churches, which had been formed as "Second Blessing" Holiness denominations, simply added the baptism in the Holy Spirit with glossolalia as "initial evidence" of a "third blessing" (Synan, 2001).

Pentecostal pioneers who had been Methodists included Charles Fox Parham, the formulator of the "initial evidence" theology; William J. Seymour, the pastor of the Azusa Street Mission in Los Angeles who spread the movement to the nations of the world; J.H. King of the Pentecostal Holiness Church, who led his denomination into the Pentecostal movement in 1907-08; and Thomas Ball Barratt, the father of European Pentecostalism. All of these men retained most of the Wesleyan teaching on Entire Sanctification as a part of their theological systems. In essence, their position was that a sanctified "clean heart" was a necessary prerequisite to the baptism in the Holy Spirit as evidenced by speaking in tongues (Synan, 2001).

Other early Pentecostal pioneers from non Methodist backgrounds accepted the premise of Second Blessing Holiness prior to becoming Pentecostals. For the most part, they were as much immersed in Holiness experience and theology as their Methodist brothers. These included C. H. Mason (Baptist) of the Church of God in Christ, A. J. Tomlinson (Quaker) of the Church of God (Cleveland, Tennessee), B.H Irwin (Baptist) of the Fire-Baptized Holiness Church, and N.J. Holmes (Presbyterian) of the Tabernacle Pentecostal Church. In the light of the foregoing information, it would not be an overstatement to say that Pentecostalism, at least in America, was born in a Holiness cradle (Synan, 2001).

Diversification of Denominational Adherents

The Pentecostal Movement is by far the largest and most important religious movement to originate in the United States. Beginning in 1901 with only a handful of students in a Bible School in Topeka, Kansas, the number of Pentecostals increased steadily throughout the world during the Twentieth Century. By 1993, they had become the largest family of Protestants in the world, with over 200,000,000 members designated as Denominational Pentecostals. This explosive growth has forced the Christian world to pay increasing attention to the entire movement and to attempt to discover the root causes of this growth (Synan, 2001).

Although the Pentecostal Movement had its beginnings in the United States, it owed much of its basic theology to earlier British Perfectionists and Charismatic Movements. At least three of these, the Methodist/Holiness Movement, the Catholic Apostolic movement of Edward Irving, and the British Keswick "Higher Life" movement, prepared the way for what appeared to be a spontaneous outpouring of the Holy Spirit in America (Synan, 2001).

Perhaps the most important immediate precursor to Pentecostalism was the Holiness Movement that issued from the heart of Methodism at the end of the Nineteenth Century. From John Wesley, the Pentecostals inherited the idea of a subsequent crisis experience variously called "Entire Sanctification," "perfect love," "Christian Perfection," or "heart purity." John Wesley posited such a possibility in his influential tract, "A Plain Account of Christian Perfection" (1766). From Wesley the Holiness Movement developed the theology of a "Second Blessing." Wesley's colleague, John Fletcher, however, was the first to call this Second Blessing a "baptism in the Holy Spirit," an experience which brought spiritual power to the recipient as well as inner cleansing. This was explained in Fletcher's major work, Checks to Antinominianism (1771). During the Nineteenth Century, thousands of Methodists claimed to receive this experience; although, no one at the time saw any connection with this spirituality and speaking in tongues or any of the other charisms (Synan, 2001).

In the following century, Edward Irving and his friends in London suggested the possibility of a restoration of the charisms in the modern church. A popular Presbyterian pastor in London, Irving led the first attempt at "charismatic renewal" in his Regents Square Presbyterian Church in 1831. Although tongues and prophecies were experienced in his church, Irving was not successful in his quest for a restoration of New Testament Christianity. In the end, the "Catholic Apostolic Church," which was founded by his followers, attempted to restore the "five-fold ministries" of apostles, prophets, evangelists, pastors, and teachers, in addition to the charisms. While his movement failed in England, Irving did succeed in pointing to glossolalia as the "standing sign" of the baptism in the Holy Spirit, a major facet in the future theology of the Pentecostals (Synan, 2001).

Another predecessor to Pentecostalism was the Keswick "Higher Life" movement which flourished in England after 1875. Led at first by American Holiness teachers such as Hannah Whitall Smith and William E. Boardman, the Keswick teachers soon changed the goal and content of the "Second Blessing" from the Wesleyan emphasis on "heart purity" to that of an "endowment of spiritual power for service." Thus, by the time of the Pentecostal outbreak in America in 1901, there had been at least a century of movements emphasizing a Second Blessing called the "baptism in the Holy Spirit" with various interpretations concerning the content and results of the experience. In America, such Keswick teachers as A.B. Simpson and A.J. Gordon also added to the movement at large with an emphasis on divine healing "as in the atonement" and the premillennial rapture of the church (Synan, 2001).

The first wave of "Azusa pilgrims" journeyed throughout the United States spreading the Pentecostal zeal, primarily in Holiness churches, missions, and camp meetings. For some time, it was thought that it was necessary to journey to California to receive the "blessing." Soon, however, people received the tongues experience wherever they lived (Synan, 2001).

American Pentecostal pioneers who received tongues at Azusa Street went back to their homes to spread the movement among their own people, at times against great opposition. One of the first was Gaston Barnabas Cashwell of North Carolina, who spoke in tongues in 1906. His six-month preaching tour of the South in 1907 resulted in major inroads among Southern Holiness adherents. Under his ministry, Cashwell saw several Holiness denominations swept into the new movement, including the Church of God (Cleveland, Tennessee), the Pentecostal Holiness Church, the Fire-Baptized Holiness Church, and the Pentecostal Free-Will Baptist Church (Synan, 2001).

Also in 1906, Charles Harrison Mason journeyed to Azusa Street and returned to Memphis, Tennessee to spread the Pentecostal fire in the Church of God in Christ. Mason and the church he founded were made up of African Americans only one generation removed from slavery (Synan, 2001).

The parents of both Seymour and Mason had been born as southern slaves. Mason in particular was a capable leader who was able to step out front and became the founder of the Church of God in Christ. Mason had been a Missionary Baptist, but left them in 1895 to join a denomination that considered themselves a Holiness movement (Synan, 2001).

Charles Price Jones, the founder of the African American Holiness Movement, was forced out of the Mount Helm Baptist church due to his boldness to embrace the doctrine of Holiness. Mason left the movement and organized the religious group now know as the Church of God in Christ. Charles Price Jones became the founder of the church organization now known as the Church of Christ Holiness U.S.A.

Mason was thus the head of an established church body before going to Azusa in 1907. Unlike Seymour, Parham, and the other

Pentecostal founders, Bishop Mason could ordain people so that they would be recognized as legitimate ministers capable of doing wedding and similar duties by civil authorities and mainstream churches. In the earliest years, Mason was the main source of ordinations for both white and black Pentecostal churches, thus leaving his mark on the entire Pentecostal movement (Longman, 2001c).

Mason's visit to Azusa was a moving moment for him: "Then I gave up for the Lord to have His way within me. So there came a wave of Glory into me and all of my being was filled with the Glory of the Lord. When I opened my mouth to say 'Glory,' a flame touched my tongue, which ran down through me. My language changed and no word could I speak in my own tongue. Oh! I was filled with the Glory of the Lord. My soul was them satisfied" (Longman 2001c, pp. 1). Having gone through that, he knew he could not continue as he was doing. He had to take it wherever he would go (Longman, 2001c).

Mason brought the new Pentecostal experience back to his churches, and many of them dived in with both feet. Other believers within Mason's present church did not receive the new doctrine and experience, including C.P. Jones, a leader within the Holiness Movement. The church split into a Holiness church and Mason's Pentecostal group. Mason, as a well-established leader, had a lot to lose by taking part in this new Pentecostal-ism. It is a tribute to the man and a mark of his following the Spirit that he made the change and took his losses in stride. His church quickly grew into a major African-American church and the largest black Pentecostal body in the nation. Mason continued to lead his church until his death in 1961 at age 95; he lived to see it become 400,000 strong. It has since grown to around five million, with no slowdown in sight (Longman, 2001c).

Other existing Holiness churches went into the early Pentecostal Movement, including the Church of God (Cleveland, TN). Their move came less because of a bold leader and more because of a full-scale grass-roots switch to the new movement. New bodies were created when congregations from a wide range of revivalist churches were swept together into new theology by the new movement.

One of the most remarkable and influential women of the early 20th century was Aimee Semple MacPherson (1890-1944). In the 1920s and 1930s, she was certainly the top woman spiritual leader of her time. She obtained a Methodist exhorters' license, started Bridal Call magazine in 1917, and became an Assemblies of God ordained minister in 1919, which she had to give up in 1922. In 1922, her preaching tour included Australia, and she drew support from an unusually wide variety of church leaders for a Pentecostal preacher. To start off the New Year in 1923, she started the Angeles Temple and formed the Foursquare churches. The "Foursquare" refers to the four facets of a vision she received, teaching Jesus as Savior, Healer, Baptizer, and Coming King, and thus creating the Foursquare emphases on salvation, divine healing, baptism in the Spirit, and preparing for the Second Coming. In 1924, she started the field of religious radio, opening station KFSG in Los Angeles. She was a major success, not only for her church, but also for the newly born radio medium. In 1927, she started the Angeles Temple Commissary, which became famous during the Great Depression for its food and other free mercies. Her lesser doctrines kept shifting around, and her personal, financial, and family life were quite a mess, but that did not stop her from inspiring millions to have confidence in God. She died in 1944 of a supposedly "accidental" overdose of pills (Longman, 2001c).

Although tongues caused a split in the church in 1907, the Church of God in Christ experienced such explosive growth that by 1993, it was by far the largest Pentecostal denomination in North America claiming some 5,500,000 members in 15,300 local churches. Another Azusa Pilgrim was William H. Durham of Chicago. After receiving his tongues experience at Azusa Street in 1907 he returned to Chicago where he led thousands of mid-western Americans and Canadians into the Pentecostal Movement. His "finished work" theology of gradual progressive sanctification, which he announced in 1910, led to the formation of the Assemblies of God in 1914. Since many white pastors had formerly been part of Mason's church, the beginnings of the Assemblies of God were also partially a racial separation. In time, the Assemblies of God church was destined to become the largest Pentecostal denominational church in the world, claiming by 1993 over 2,000,000 members in the U.S. and some 25,000,000 adherents in 150 nations of the world (Synan, 2001).

In addition to the ministers who received their Pentecostal experience at Azusa Street, thousands were indirectly influenced by the revival in Los Angeles. Among these was Thomas Ball Barratt of Norway, a Methodist pastor later to be known as the Pentecostal apostle to Northern and Western Europe. Receiving a glossolalic baptism in the Spirit in New York City in 1906, he returned to Oslo where he conducted the first Pentecostal services in Europe in December of 1906. From Norway, Barratt traveled to Sweden, England, France, and Germany where he sparked other national Pentecostal movements. Under Barratt such leaders as Lewi Pethrus in Sweden, Jonathan Paul in Germany, and Alexander Boddy in England were brought into the movement (Synan, 2001).

From Chicago, through the influence of William Durham, the movement spread quickly to Italy and South America. Two Italian immigrants to Chicago, Luigi Francescon and Giacomo Lombardy founded thriving Italian Pentecostal movements after 1908 in the U.S.A., Brazil, Argentina, and Italy. Also, in South Bend, Indiana (near Chicago) two Swedish Baptist immigrants, Daniel Berg and Gunnar Vingren, received the Pentecostal experience and felt a prophetic call to Brazil. Their missionary trip in 1910 resulted in the formation of the Brazilian Assemblies of God, which developed into the largest national Pentecostal Movement in the world, claiming some 15,000,000 members by 1993. Also hailing from Chicago was Willis C. Hoover, the Methodist missionary to Chile who in 1909 led a Pentecostal revival in the Chilean Methodist Episcopal Church. After being excommunicated from the Methodist Episcopal Church, Hoover and 37 of his followers organized the "Pentecostal Methodist Church" which by 1993 grew to number some 1,500,000 adherents in Chile (Synan, 2001).

African Pentecostalism owed its origins to the work of John Graham Lake (1870-1935) who began his ministry as a Methodist preacher but later prospered in the business world as an insurance executive. In 1898, his wife was miraculously healed of tuberculosis under the ministry of divine healer Alexander Dowie, founder of a religious community called "Zion City" near Chicago, Illinois. Joining with Dowie, Lake became an elder in the "Zion Catholic Apostolie Church." At one point, Lake testified to an instant experience of Entire Sanctification in the home of Fred Bosworth, an early leader in the Assemblies of God. In 1907, he received the Pentecostal experience and spoke in tongues under the ministry of Charles Parham, who visited Zion while the aging Dowie was losing control of his ministry. Out of Zion also came a host of almost 500 preachers who entered the ranks of the Pentecostal Movement, chief of whom was John G. Lake (Synan, 2001.

After his Pentecostal experience, Lake abandoned the insurance business in order to answer a long-standing call to minister in South Africa. In April 1908, he led a large missionary party to Johannesburg where he began to spread the Pentecostal message throughout the nation. Coming with him was his wife and seven children as well as Holiness evangelists Thomas Hezmalhalch and J.C. Lehman. Only Lehman had been to Africa before in 1908, having served for five years as a missionary to the Zulus. Hezmalhalch, lovingly known as "Brother Tom," was born in England and was sixty years of age when he arrived in South Africa. Before the end of his first year in South Africa, Lake's wife died, some believed due to malnutrition. Lake nevertheless succeeded in founding two large and influential Pentecostal churches in South Africa. The white branch took the name "Apostolic Faith Mission" (AFM) in 1910, borrowed from the name of the famous mission on Azusa Street. This church eventually gave David DuPlessis to the world as "Mr. Pentecost." The Black branch eventually developed into the "Zion Christian Church" (ZCC) which by 1993 claimed no fewer than 6,000,000 members and, despite some doctrinal and cultural variations, was recognized as the largest Christian church in the nation. In its annual Easter conference at Petersburg, this church gathers upwards of 2,000,000 worshippers, the largest annual gathering of Christians on earth (Synan, 2001).

After his African missionary tour of 1908-1912, Lake returned to the United States where he founded churches and healing homes in Spokane, Washington and Portland, Oregon before his death in 1935. Throughout the rest of the century, Pentecostal denominational missionaries from many nations spread the movement to all parts of Africa. In addition to the AFM and ZCC churches, the Pentecostal Holiness Church in South Africa was founded in 1913 under the leadership of Lehman who had come with Lake in 1908. In 1917, the Assemblies of God entered South Africa when the American church accepted the mission already established by R.M. Turney. The Church of God (Cleveland, Tennessee) came to the country in 1951 through amalgamation with the Full Gospel Church. In retrospect, the work of Lake was the most influential and enduring of all the South African Pentecostal mission endeavors (Synan, 2001).

Soon after Lake returned to the United States, the movement reached the Slavic world through the ministry of a Russian-born Baptist pastor, Ivan Voronaev who received the Pentecostal experience in New York City in 1919. Through prophecies, he was led to take his family with him to Odessa in the Ukraine in 1922 where he established the first Pentecostal church in the Soviet Union. Although he was arrested, imprisoned, and martyred in a communist prison in 1943, Voronaev's churches survived incredible persecution to become a major religious force in Russia and the former Soviet Union (Synan, 2001).

This first wave of Pentecostal pioneer missionaries produced what has become known as the "Classical Pentecostal Movement" with over 1,000 Pentecostal denominations throughout the world. These continued to proliferate at an amazing rate as the century came to an end. In retrospect, the pattern established in South Africa was repeated in man other nations as the movement spread around the world. That is, an enterprising Pentecostal pioneer, such as Lake, broke the ground for a new movement which was initially despised and rejected by the existing churches. This phase was followed by organized Pentecostal denominational mission efforts that produced fast-growing missions and indigenous churches. The final phase was the penetration of Pentecostalism into the mainline Protestant and Catholic churches as "charismatic renewal" Movements with the aim of renewing and reviving the historic churches. Strangely enough, these newer "waves" also originated largely in the United States. These included the Protestant "Neo-Pentecostal" Movement that began in 1960 in Van Nuys, California under the ministry of Dennis Bennett, Rector of St. Marks Episcopal (Anglican) Church (Synan, 2001).

Within a decade, this movement had spread to all the 150 major Protestant families of the world reaching a total of 55,000,000 people by 1990. The Catholic Charismatic Renewal Movement had its beginnings in Pittsburgh, Pennsylvania in 1967 among students and faculty of DuQuesne University. Added to these is the newest category, the "Third Wave" of the Spirit that originated at Fuller Theological Seminary in 1981 under the classroom ministry of John Wimber. These consisted of mainline Evangelicals who moved in signs and wonders. but who disdained labels such as "Pentecostal" or "charismatic." By 1990 this group numbered some 33,000,000 members in the world (Synan, 2001).

The two movements, both Pentecostal and Charismatic, have come to constitute a major force in Christendom throughout the world with explosive growth rates not seen before in modern times. By 1990, the Pentecostals and their charismatic brothers and sisters in the mainline Protestant and Catholic churches were turning their attention toward world evangelization. Only time will tell and reveal the ultimate results of these movements which have greatly impacted the world during the Twentieth Century.

CHAPTER 5

MAJOR CONTRIBUTIONS OF THE HOLINESS FAITH

The Holiness Movement contributed to a richer spiritual life in a materialistic age. The Holiness Movement encouraged Christian believers in America to grow closer to their personal walk with God and pursue their religious commitment to new levels. At the heart of religious practices in America was prayer. Prayer was crucial because it facilitated a deeper appreciation for the religious agenda. The time was ripe for a greater zeal and dialogue on the matter of religion intervention to impact the social and moral welfare of the nation. The Holiness Movement was the key that opened new avenues of growth and expansion within the Christian faith during the Twentieth Century.

America had always been a religious country, but the Holiness Movement encouraged key religious leaders to embrace a higher calling in God. The movement ignited a hunger within believers that reached new levels of religious involvement.

Deepening of Spritual Life

During Holiness camp meetings, testimonies were given that confirmed that the practice of religion and Holiness principles have beneficial effects on behavior and social relations, such as illegitimacy, crime and delinquency, social dependency, alcohol and drug abuse, suicide, depression, and general self-esteem. The champions of Holiness doctrine encouraged its followers to embrace a higher standard in God and their teaching challenged followers to move to a higher plain. Following biblical teaching became one of the most powerful factors in preventing out-of-wedlock births as the members of the Holiness faith practiced their religious beliefs

Even in today's efforts to curve the practice of sex before marriage and teenage pregnancy, it has long been known that intensity of religious practice is closely related to adolescent virginity, sexual restraint, and control. This general finding, replicated again and again, also holds true specifically for black teenage girls, the group with the highest teen pregnancy rates among all demographic subgroups. Without exception, religious practice sharply reduces the incidence of premarital intercourse. The reverse is also true. The absence of religious practice accompanies sexual permissiveness and premarital sex (Fagan, 1996).

The impact of religious practice on teenage sexual behavior also can be seen at the state level. In an important study published in 1987, a group of professors from the Universities of Georgia, Utah, and Wyoming found that the main cause of problematic adolescent sexual behaviors and attitudes is not only family dynamics and processes, as previously thought, but also the absence of religious behavior and affiliation. They further concluded that healthy family dynamics and practices are themselves affected to a powerful degree by the presence or absence of religious beliefs and practices. The same results also hold true in international comparisons (Fagan, 1996).

In 1991, David Larson, adjunct professor at the Northwestern and Duke University Schools of Medicine and president of the National Institute of Healthcare Research, completed a systematic review of studies on religious commitment and personal well-being. He found that the relationship is powerful and positive; overall, psychological functioning improved following a resumption of participation in religious worship for those who had stopped (Fagan, 1996).

The Establishment of Religious Organizations

Since many of the Pentecostal revivals started as a result of Holiness teaching, the importance of Holiness doctrine cannot be minimized. The Holiness faith was the platform that launched other movements and had a significant impact on religious diversification.

In February of 1906, a Holiness church without a pastor decided to hear out William Seymour, a preacher recommended by members Neely Terry and Julia Hutchins. However, once Seymour arrived in Los Angeles, he raised the matter of speaking in tongues, which Seymour had come to see as the definitive mark of the entry of the Holy Spirit into a person. As a result, Seymour was bounced even before he could get started. Seymour held his meetings at the home of Richard and Ruth Asberry. The meetings drew some of the exiles from the First and Second Baptist churches and a few from nearby Holiness churches. These meetings already had some of Seymour's trademarks. They were interracial and involved women, and lay people exercised leadership and specialized gifts (Longman, 2001a).

On April 9, 1906, Edward Lee, who was housing Seymour, and Jennie Evans Moore, Seymour's closest associate, experienced speaking in tongues. Others soon followed. News traveled fast as

Seymour's group gained attention within the community. The group eventually rented an abandoned warehouse on Azusa Street that was previously used as a livery stable, and they started the Apostolic Faith Mission. Things shifted into high gear on Easter when Moore gave her testimony. The news was also about "prophecies" and apocalyptic visions that predicted calamity, right before a major earthquake hit California (Longman, 2001a).

In May of 1906, the mission was already overflowing their new site. The Pentecostal movement was born. Visiting pastors came from everywhere, especially from the South. Reporters from secular newspapers were sent to check out the scene. All eyes were on Azusa in a matter of weeks. The unusually popular news traveled speedily across the country, at a time before there were modern media and passenger airlines, and the telecommunications revolution had barely begun (Longman, 2001a).

Seymour was not what most people would think of as a black Pentecostal preacher. He was usually a meek man with a straightforward style. He saw himself more as a teacher than a preacher, yet his mark was as a preacher and not as a teacher. He would sometimes sit at the meetings with his head in a shoe box, to cut himself off from the hysteria surrounding him, apparently for two reasons: (1) to keep from becoming visually disoriented, as he was blind in one eye, and (2) so he could concentrate on prayer and thought, so that he would be most open to speaking in the Spirit. The people in attendance were already in a state of excited agitation long before Seymour spoke, due to what went on before him each night. When his powerful influence impacted the community, it was more than most people could take (Longman, 2001a).

While most of the elders and the pastor kept themselves relatively straight, the scene which revolved around Azusa was increasingly under the sway of magicians, self-appointed preachers, self-styled prophets, and folk religionists, who would repulse any Holiness devotee such as Parham, or for that matter any sincere Christian. They also triggered most of Seymour's biggest eruptions (Longman, 2001a).

This water/oil mix of Parham and Azusa was the first sign of something that would plague Pentecostalism and become a part of its character: divisiveness. Two other problems that would infect Pentecostalism showed themselves here: fraud and the influence of occult mysticism. Parham himself was an example of three other problems that would recur throughout Pentecostal history: racism, authoritarianism, and sexual scandal. Also, one of the troubles with going by exciting experiences is that much of what went on was not thought through as thoroughly as was needed. So, not only were the glories of Pentecostalism born at Azusa, but also serious problems of moral reproach (Longman, 2001a).

Prior to the end of 1906, most Azusa leaders had spun off to form congregations, such as the 51st Street Apostolic Faith Mission, the Spanish AFM, and the Italian Pentecostal Mission. These missions were made up mostly of some immigrant or ethnic group. The U.S. Southeast was a particularly fruitful area for them, since Azusa's approach gave a useful explanation for things that had already been happening there in fact or in rumor. Other new missions were based on preachers who had charisma or energy. Nearly all of these new churches were founded among the poor, the outcast, the newcomer, and/or the low wage laborer (Longman, 2001a).

It appeared that the influence of the Azusa Street experience had started shrinking. The good news was that once people had stopped paying attention to Azusa, those who were there for the experience had left. Azusa was eventually able to straighten itself out and settle itself into being a black Pentecostal church not all that different from others, doing a brief resurgence and then a slow fade into conservatism. The bad new was that the con artists found as many places elsewhere to go as the Pentecostal Movement had found, causing continued problems for the more legitimate leaders (Longman, 2001a).

The congregation at Azusa continued at a reasonable size until Seymour's death in 1922, at which time Jennie Moore Seymour took over for several years of decline. The congregation dispersed soon after losing its building in 1931. The building was torn down and replaced by what became the Japanese-American Cultural and Community Center in Los Angeles (Longman, 2001a).

In a way, the congregation's demise was fitting, for the Pentecostal Movement has thrived on temporary sites, storefronts, old warehouses, and on congregations that often would last not much past their chief preacher. The constant shifting has made it harder for rigor mortis to set in, and has kept them open to new possibilities in changing neighborhoods (Longman, 2001a).

Even though the stratification of the Holiness Movement has its history with many religious groups, it still carries the legacy of creating the fire and drive that kept the passion alive and led the way toward the continual evolvement of church growth into many world renowned religious organizations. The Holiness Movement left a mark on many schools of thought. The results of what happened at Azusa Street were crucial in the establishment of the New Order of Latter Rain Movement. George Hawtin organized the Latter Rain Movement in Canada. The Salvation - Healing Movement is given credit to William Branham, who had been given what by all accounts were a spectacular personal ministry of healing, and the work of several successors, such as Gordon Lindsey and Oral Roberts. Leaders such as Kenneth Copeland, Ken Hagin, and Ulf Ekman, known for the Word of Faith Movement, are considered to be very popular. All of these are a cross breed of Pentecostalism with the New Thought Movement which gave birth to Unity School and Christian Science. The above leaders were all crucial in carrying the doctrine of Holiness to new levels.

All Holiness Churches are Trinitarian, Arminian (free will, not Calvinist), and teach Entire Sanctification, which states you can be sinless in this life. Sin is willful disobedience as opposed to just missing the mark. They do not recognize the possibility of an unknown sin (Leviticus 4:2).

The following is a list of Wesleyan Holiness denominations:

- The Apostolic Christian Church of America was organized in 1847. Women in the membership did not wear open-arm garments or take oaths and the clergy are not paid. According to their history clergy did not outline sermons but relied on the Holy Spirit for their leading.
- The Apostolic Faith Church was founded 1907. The beliefs were a mixture of Holiness and Pentecostal teaching. They banned activities such as dance, alcohol, smoking, playing cards, visiting the theater, and forbade marrying unbelievers. They dress conservatively.
- The Apostolic Overcoming Holy Church of God was founded 1916. Some Holiness and Pentecostals followers accepted as women clergy but banned activities such as smoking, foolish talking, jesting, slang, and marrying unbelievers.
- Church of Christ (Holiness) U.S.A. The first Holiness convention was called in 1897. Followers believed in divine healing, strong eschatological focus, and foot washing. They banned activities such as dance, alcohol, smoking, playing cards, visiting the theater and secret societies.

THE HOLINESS EXPERIENCE AND ITS EVOLUTION

- Church of God (Holiness) was founded 1886. The membership banned activities such as dance, alcohol, smoking, playing cards, theater, and marrying unbelievers. Members were asked not to wear short-sleeve shirts or ties. Divorcing your current spouse to remarry your first spouse was encouraged.
- The Church of the Nazarene was founded 1908. The church banned such activities as dancing, alcohol, smoking, theater and membership in secret societies.
- The Churches of Christ in Christian Union was founded 1909.
- The International Pentecostal Holiness Church was founded in 1911. Church members believed in Holiness teaching, Pentecostal pre-millennial and divine healing.
- The Wesleyan Church founded 1843. They believed in Holiness and banned drinking alcohol, smoking and membership in secret societies.

Methodist churches:

- The African Methodist Episcopal Church was founded 1814. They believed in Holiness and women clergy. It is a black church.
- The African Methodist Episcopal Zion Church was founded 1821
- The Christian Methodist Episcopal Church was founded 1870.
- The Congregational Methodist Church was founded 1852.
- The Evangelical Church of North America was founded 1968.
- The Evangelical Congregational Church was founded 1894.

- The Evangelical Methodist Church was founded 1946.
- The Free Methodist Church of North America was founded 1860. Church followers believed in Holiness teaching and banned activities, such as membership in secret societies.
- The Pillar of fire was founded 1901. They believed in Holiness, pre-millennialism, and banned membership in secret societies.
- The Primitive Methodist Church, USA was founded 1840.
- The Southern Methodist Church was founded 1939.
- The United Methodist Church was founded 1968. The organization believed in Holiness teaching and women clergy.

The complex interaction of religion and society must be analyzed to understand the rise of new religious consciousness during any particular time-period. One form of religious expression must be related to another, and the entire spectrum of religious institutions and ideology must be linked to the society as a whole. Unfortunately, most standard, historical, and contemporary accounts of religious change examine individual religious groups without analyzing the social context out of which they emerged (Glock, Bellah, 1976).

Since the current flourishing of new religious sects is by no means unique in American history, a historical perspective of religious transformation provides an opportunity to analyze the relationship between religion and social change (Glock, Bellah, 1976).

Moral and Spiritual Implications

The available evidence clearly demonstrates that regular religious practice is both an individual and social good. It is a powerful answer to many of our most significant social problems, some of which, including out-of-wedlock births, have reached catastrophic proportions. Furthermore, it is available to all, and at no cost.

Holiness teaching was instrumental in causing Americans to become aware of the fundamental contribution that married family life and regular religious practice can make to preserve their society. The practice of Holiness teaching was good for individuals, families, states, and the nation. It improves health, learning, economic well being, self-control, self-esteem, and empathy. It reduces the incidence of social pathologies, such as out-of-wedlock births, crime, delinquency, drug and alcohol addiction, health problems, anxieties, and prejudices (Fagan, 1996).

Holiness teaching helped pave the way toward the support of women's rights and educated the public on the mistreatment of black Americans. It was important that Congress promoted the freedom of all Americans to practice their religious beliefs.

The widespread practice of religious beliefs benefited the nation, and the task of reintegrating religious practice into American life while protecting and respecting the rights of non-practice—rights that, despite persistent demagoguery on the subject, remain totally unthreatened—are some of the nation's most important tasks. Academics of good will can do much in this area, and history will look kindly on those who help America achieve this wonderful balance (Fagan, 1996).

When American Methodism was formed in 1784, the church accepted Wesley's mandate to reform the continent and spread Scriptural Holiness over these lands. For over a century, Methodist preachers and churches throughout the nation promoted the Holiness cause.

As the church grew larger and wealthier, the Holiness testimony tended to fade as a distinctive teaching and experience in the church. Despite attempts to renew the Holiness message in the church both before and after the Civil War, the trend away from Holiness theology and experience was clearly established by the end of the Nineteenth Century.

The last major revival among Methodist and other mainline Protestant churches came after the formation of the National Holiness Association in the state of New Jersey, in 1867. The resulting revival failed to bring the majority of the American church back to the Holiness cause. When the Southern Methodist Church rejected the Holiness Movement in 1894, over 25 new Holiness groups dedicated to the promotion of Holiness preaching and living were formed in the United States.

As a result of their many differences, the Pentecostal Church began after 1904 as a result of the controversies over the questions of sanctification and spiritual gifts. As a result of many differences, the Pentecostal Holiness Church Movement separated itself from Methodist influences and forged its own destiny.

CHAPTER 6

THE HAND OF GOD THAT DIRECT RELIGIOUS HISTORY

According to the Bible, God's involvement in human history began as soon as Adam and Eve were created. God commanded Adam and Eve to subdue the earth (Gen. 1: 27-28). His continual involvement is evident as He directed the forces that continue to change and shape world events today (Psalms 24:1-2).

God's involvement did not end with the creation of the world. His intervention continued to impact not only societal events but also religious theology. The Holiness Movement impacted America and caused many changes in religious doctrine that originated in North America. The Holiness Movement gave rise to a new religious agenda within America. Holiness theology is responsible for changing religious platforms everywhere, as differences in biblical interpretation continued to arise.

The emergence of the Holiness Movement was not by chance. God moved upon the hearts and minds of religious followers who brought about a new order of religious expressions that challenged religious doctrine within America.

The experience at Azusa brought about a wave of religious experience that forged what is now known as the Pentecostal Experience. Even though this experience did not originate within the Pentecostal Church, it was enough to brand many Pentecostal groups. Some Protestant followers believed that the experience failed to embrace the full truth of the Gospel found in the New Testament teachings.

In spite of the many differences that occurred as a result of the Pentecostal experience, God allowed the expansion and evolvement of religious doctrine in the world. The change challenged America and ignited religious interest everywhere. According to the Bible "all things work together for good to them that love God" (Romans S: 28).

Protestant Theology and God's Intervention

The world has come to the reality that there are three branches of religious theology: Catholic, Protestant, and Pentecostal. Pentecostalism itself is not a denomination, but a rapidly growing religious phenomenon among all major sections of Christendom. Religious commentators are beginning to recognize it as the third force in the Christian world (Slade n.d.).

Sometimes called the "Charismatic Movement," it is no longer confined to the small Pentecostal groups as it once was. This movement is becoming quite widespread within the Catholic Church as well as the more conservative Protestant denominations. It can be identified by the experience of speaking in tongues, or glossolalia (Slade n.d.).

Interdenominational groups, like the Full Gospel Business Men's Fellowship International, are very active in spreading the "Pentecostal baptism of the Spirit." So many charismatic groups are springing up, especially in the younger generation, that this movement has been dubbed the "Jesus Revolution" (Slade n.d.).

Most Protestant followers feel that the Pentecostal experience lacks the New Testament emphasis on repentance, faith, and obedience. Even in the realm of subjective experience in the Gospel, Pentecostalism fails to place the primary emphasis where the New Testament places it on repentance, faith and obedience (Slade n.d.).

Jesus commanded His disciples to preach repentance and faith. Paul preached "repentance toward God, and faith toward our Lord Jesus Christ" (Acts 20:21).

Repentance means a godly sorrow for sin. The heart will never experience this unless it becomes sensible of its own moral defilement in the light of God's law (Slade n.d.).

The majesty, Holiness, and justice of God must be presented in order to prick the heart and mind of the sinner until he/she sees something of how offensive and damning is his/her state of corruption and rebellion in the sight of Infinite Purity. When the sharp arrows of conviction pierce the soul and the sinner becomes terrified with the thought of appearing before God in his/her sin, then the soul is ready to hear the good news of God's saving love in Jesus Christ. The message of the cross does not lessen the sense of sin, but deepens it, for in the light of the terrible suffering of the Savior the sinner sees how grievous sin appears in God's sight (Slade n.d.).

By the working of the Spirit upon his/her heart, the sinner begins to hate sin for what it is and longs for that purity and righteousness which the sinner is powerless to attain. The Spirit not only gives him/her repentance toward God for breaking His law, but also faith in the Lord Jesus Christ. This faith is not a mere opinion about the historical Jesus, but it is a trusting response of the whole life of Jesus Christ. The repentant sinner, claiming no merit of his/her own, comes into the presence of a holy God presenting nothing but the merits of a crucified and risen Savior, claiming nothing except that Christ stands as his/her substitute (Slade n.d.).

True faith will bring forth the fruit of obedience to the whole will of God, to the whole law of God. Faith is the seed or root of obedience because it acknowledges the lordship of Jesus Christ over the whole life. The primary graces imparted by the Holy Spirit are repentance, faith, and obedience. The wondering crowd will be more enamored and impressed with spectacular things, like miracles and tongues. A circus is more pleasing to carnal hearts than self-renunciation, sorrow for sin, and faith that will be manifested in obedience to all the commandments of God (Slade n.d.).

Pentecostal Experience is based on subjective experience rather than on the objective Word of God. Apostle Paul writes, "Faith cometh by hearing, and hearing by the Word of God" (Rom. 10:17). Faith does not rest on one's experience, however elevating and Spirit filled that experience might be. Salvation rests entirely on Death and resurrection, just as Isaiah says, "By His knowledge shall my righteous Servant justify many" (Isaiah. 53:11). And the apostle Paul declares, "By the obedience of one shall many be made righteous" (Rom. 5:19). It cannot be stressed too strongly that Bible faith rests upon something that was done entirely outside of man. The Word of God instructs the sinner in the knowledge of Christ's infinitely perfect character, His infinite sacrifice on the cross, and His triumphant resurrection (Slade n.d.).

This knowledge of what God has done for mankind creates faith in the sinner's heart. Faith rests on the certainty of that objective salvation, feeling or no feeling. If the believer feels sinful and destitute of the Spirit, he may still rest in the fact that Christ died for the ungodly. If he is filled with the Spirit and transported to the mountain-top of Christian experience, he still knows that his experience cannot save him or recommend him to God (Slade n.d.).

The Pentecostal will say that seeing believes. But subjective experience is no criterion for truth. A true Christian must live by every word that proceeds out of the mouth of God (Luke 4:4). According to the Bible, man must not judge after the sight of his eyes or after the hearing of his ears (Isaiah 11:3). Remember that Jesus said, "many would come in His name and show great signs and wonders, and if possible deceive the very elect" (Matt. 24:24). The Bible says that, "in the last days Satan will work with all sins and power and lying wonders" (2 Thessalonians 2:9). In the last judgment many will come to Christ, saying, "Lord, Lord, have we not done many wonderful works?" But Jesus will say, "Depart from me, ye that work iniquity" (Matt. 7:22, 23).

Searching of the Word of God for light and truth is needed in the world today. By the utterances of the Bible, every experience and miracle must be tested. If we trust in our senses, we shall surely be deceived. If man trusts his experience, he merits the condemnation of fools, for it is written, "He that trust in his own heart is a fool" (Proverbs 28:26). A constant danger exists that religious enthusiasts will mistake their whims and impulses as the Holy Spirit, when in reality they are the promptings of the wayward human heart (Slade n.d.).

The Holiness faith believes strongly on the "Agape" love of the New Testament. They feel that it is not a sentiment of emotion, but a heaven-born principle.

Pentecostal doctrine presents love as a rapture or feeling that is enjoyed in the believer's heart. The Bible presents love as a principle of unselfish concern for others. These two concepts are as different as night is from day (Slade n.d.).

In embracing the Pentecostal experience the believer is normally expected to do things because the "love" in his heart makes him feel like doing it. He may even quote Paul, who says, "The love of Christ constraineth us" (II Corinthians 5:14). The one who accepts the principle of Bible love will do things whether he/she feels like doing them or not. In fact, in the matter of duty, his/her feelings will not even be consulted. The believer's first concern is God's glory, and he/she will obey Him even if it runs contrary to his/her own feelings and impulses. The believer will keep God's law at the expense of personal convenience or even life itself. He/she will do this because he/she has made Jesus first, last, and best in everything. Furthermore, he/she will serve and seek to benefit his/her fellow men. The believer may not have a strong emotional feeling toward them. He/she may not like some of them. But he/she will love them, as souls for whom Christ died (Slade n.d.).

Pentecostal Theology and Spiritual Gifts

Some Pentecostal followers oppose Protestant positions regarding religious experience. Pentecostal experience was born out of the zeal of believers who sought to embrace a deeper relationship with God. Therefore the teachings to desire spiritual Gifts were the norm within the religious community during the early 19th century.

The ministry of spiritual gifts is recognized in the Old and New Testament, commissioned by our Lord. After He established His church on the earth and ascended to Heaven, Jesus sent the Holy Spirit to equip His church with power and spiritual gifts, so that His disciples could continue to carry out His ministry objectives. While there are certain gifts of a spectacular nature that are often given greater attention, the New Testament mentions at least 21 that are provided to the church. These gifts are listed in Eph. 4:11, Rom.

12:3-7, and 1 Cor. 12:1-12, 28 and they are generally assigned to one of three categories, as listed below: Ministry (office) gifts: apostle, prophet, evangelist, pastor and teacher. Motivational (practical) gifts: service, exhortation, giving, leadership, mercy, helps and administration. Charismatic (spiritual) gifts: wisdom, knowledge, discernment, prophecy, tongues, interpretation, faith, healing and miracles (Robins 1995).

Most churches and denominations accept some variation of the motivational and ministry gifts, perhaps with controversy over the office of apostle and prophet. However, others completely reject the modern day operation of the nine charismatic gifts listed in 1Cor. 12:1-12. In brief, their view is taken from an interpretation of 1Cor 13:8-10, claiming that such spectacular gifts were only intended as a short-lived, supernatural lift to help the early church get started that they vanished after the last apostles of Jesus died (Robbins, 1995).

Charismatic gifts in church history clearly refute any notion that charismatic gifts faded away after the apostolic era. Other than diminishing somewhat during the middle Ages (probably due to the inaccessibility of Scripture to the common people), it is obvious that spiritual gifts were never completely absent from the church. Scores of statements to this effect were recorded by church leaders such as Irenaeus, who wrote around A.D. 150, "... we hear many of the brethren in the church who have prophetic gifts, and who speak in tongues through the spirit, and who also bring to light the secret things of men for their benefit." Near the close of the second century, Tertullian cited similar incidents, describing the operation of prophecies, healings and tongues, and in 210 A.D., Origin reported many healings, and other charismatic gifts, as did later writers such as Eusebius, Firmilian, Chrysostom and others throughout many centuries (Robbins, 1995).

In recent years, a mighty outpouring of the Holy Spirit brought about what was called the "Pentecostal Movement" in the early 1900's, when many churches experienced a revival of the Holy Spirit's power and spiritual gifts. Later in the 1960's spiritual gifts began to emerge in all kinds of churches and mainline denominations throughout the world, in what was called the "charismatic renewal." Spiritual gifts were suddenly manifested wherever believers or congregations were receptive and opened themselves to the inner workings of the Holy Spirit (Robbins, 1995).

Today, the spiritual gifts remain available as a part of God's plan for His church, and they are increasingly being manifested among believers around the world.

They are sometimes called God's "power tools," given to the bod of Christ as valuable helps to accomplish works of ministry (Robbins, 1995).

According to I Corinthians 12:7, "the manifestation of the Spirit is given to each one for the profit of all:

> (12:8) for to one is given the word of wisdom through the Spirit, to another the word of knowledge through the same Spirit, (12:9) to another faith by the same Spirit, to another gifts of healings by the same Spirit,

> (12:10) to another the working of miracles, to another prophecy, to another discerning of spirits, to another different kinds of tongues, to another the interpretation of tongues. (12:11) But one and the same Spirit works all these things, distributing to each one individually as He wills."

These above gifts might be well defined as a temporary, supernatural intervention of natural laws, bestowed by the Holy Spirit where His presence is invited and accommodated. Individually, each gift is defined as follows:

- Word of wisdom – A word of wisdom refers to a supernaturally imparted fragment, while wisdom, generally refers to prudence, making.
- Word of knowledge – A supernaturally inspired utterance of facts.
- Faith – A supernatural impartation of assurance in God.
- Gift of healing – supernaturally ministering health to the sick
- Working of miracles – A supernatural intervention of natural laws. The Greek describes it as "works of power" and implies instantaneous results.
- Prophecy – A supernaturally inspired utterance from God. A genuine prophetic utterance never contradicts, nor is equal to, the written Word of God. It consisted of foretelling the future and speaking from the mind of God. Prophecies are to be judged (1 Corinthians 14:29, 1 Thessalonians 5:20-21).
- Discerning of spirits – A supernatural ability to discern a person's spiritual character and the source of his actions and messages, such as from the Holy Spirit, demonic spirits, the human spirit or from the flesh.
- Different kinds of tongues – A supernaturally imparted utterance in an unknown language interpreted as a prophecy to the body for their edification. This is distinguished from "praying" in tongues, which is intended to edify one's own spirit – 1 Corinthians 14:14. A message in tongues to the

body is always to be interpreted (by another gift and is limited to three within a gathering (1 Corinthians 14:27).
- Interpretation of tongues – The supernatural interpretation of a message in tongues into the understandable language of the hearers. It is not a "translation," but an interpretation (Robbins, 1995).

One should always remember that the purpose of all the gifts is to edify the church, and their distribution within the body is completely dependent upon the discretion of the Holy Spirit (1 Corinthians 12:11). The Scriptures imply that it is appropriate to seek specific gifts (I Corinthians 14:1); however, one's motive must be for the building up of the church, not for self-gratification. "Since you are zealous for spiritual gifts, let it be for the edification of the church that you seek to excel" (1 Corinthians 14:12) (Robbins, 1995).

Spiritual gifts and spiritual fruit are not the same. Gifts are the Spirit's manifestation through a vessel, while spiritual fruit is the offspring of one's spiritual character. Spirituality cannot be measured by gifts, but by fruit (Gal. 5:22-24). Love is the predominant feature of spirituality (1 Corinthians 13:13), without which charismatic gifts cannot function effectively (1 Corinthians 13:1-2). Paul expressed that the church should have a desire for spiritual gifts, but it should follow the foremost pursuit of love (1 Corinthians 14:1) (Robbins, 1995).

Worship services where spiritual gifts function may take on a less structured, more spontaneous environment, which may seem peculiar to some. But in 1 Corinthians 14, the apostle Paul established specific guidelines for their use in order to remove the potential for confusion and disorder. Rather than banishing the operation of these gifts entirely as some churches have done in fear of disorder, they should seek to understand and implement the prescribed order, as the apostle Paul admonished: "Therefore,

THE HOLINESS EXPERIENCE AND ITS EVOLUTION

brethren, desire earnestly to prophesy, and do not forbid to speak with tongues. Let all things be done decently and in order" (1 Corinthians 14:39-40) (Robbins, 1995).

Even though much controversy resulted as the Pentecostal Movement stratified itself, God allowed its influence to forever change the Christian view regarding religion. History reveals God's providence reshaping the religious fiber of the church world. The power of God's intervention made its way into mainline Protestant churches and across denominational lines.

Catholic, Protestant, and Orthodox theology have far too long overlooked the fact that the Pentecostal movements have become a spiritual and political force. Whereas the membership of the traditional churches is declining, that of the Pentecostal churches is rising all over the world. From the insignificant beginnings of a black community on Azusa Street, Los Angeles, these churches have now developed into a mass movement with several million adherents, represented also, and particularly, in great urban centers from New York to Mexico City, and to Seoul. By contrast, Europe has largely remained untouched by this Charismatic Movement (Moltmann, 1993).

Today a generation of Pentecostals has grown up which need not be afraid of comparisons with the theology of the traditional churches in academic discussion or in exegetical and systematic development of the faith. The establishment of universities and seminaries, the founding of journals and the production of theological literature from the Pentecostal Movement represent nothing less than an offer of dialogue and co-operation in the conflicting fields of a Christian ecumene. Indeed, the perhaps surprising result of our dialogue volume is that there are only a few fundamental differences between the traditional churches and the new Pentecostal churches, and there are many common factors (Moltmann, 1993).

GEORGE A. MILLER

The Unity of Holiness and Pentecostal Doctrine

Unification among Christians is crucial to the growth and expansion of the church organizations today. The Word of God says that, "there is one Lord, one faith, and one baptism" (Ephesians 4:5). Two affirmations about the Christian Church on which almost all Christians would agree are as follows: (1) God's church is one, and (2) His church is holy. To question these statements would be to contradict the expressed wishes of Jesus in John 17, to disregard the churchly metaphors of the apostle Paul, and to ignore declarations about the Church by most of the other New Testament writers. So when any follower of Christ announces that he/she believes in the unity and sanctity of the Church, he/she creates little excitement, evokes almost no argument, and finds few challengers (Smith n.d.).

Once the affirmations are made, however, there comes the added task of elaborating their meaning. Here the complications and difficulties begin and continue. The problem is perhaps best identified and simplified in the reported conversation between two sectarians in which one concedingly said to the other, "After all, when we get down to basics, each of us is earnestly striving to do the will of the Lord, you in your way and I in His." The result is a severely fractured "body of Christ," a blemished "bride" with spots and wrinkles and other such things, and multiple "buildings" made with human hands (Smith n.d.).

Believers are aware of the divided state of Christen-dom. We are all too well aware of the hundreds of sects and denominations that cluster under separate labels and banners. Believers also recognize the fact that most Christians are neither repentant nor apologetic about these distinctions. Indeed, they are not only willing but also proud to wear a name tag that separates them from other Christians and, in effect, says, "Thank God, I'm not as others are!" (Smith n.d.).

Yet, in the context of such universal acceptance of the ideal of Christian unity, there is certain discomfiture about this separateness. This is not a recent development. Uneasiness about division in the Church goes all the way back to the first century. Much of the development of creeds and structures in the primitive and medieval periods of Christian history was specifically aimed at solving the problem of disunity (Smith n.d.).

The sixteenth-century Reformers, likewise, were not unmindful of the charge that in separating from the Roman church they were guilty of schism. In order to live with their own consciences, both Luther and Calvin were compelled to develop their own internal rationale for separating from Catholicism. Luther eased his mind by declaring that the papal institution was apostate and had actually ceased to be the Church as early as the eighth century, so in departing from it he reasoned that he was not really dividing the Church. Calvin utilized the ancient Augustinian argument against the Donatists, who objected to sinners in the Church. The Invisible Church, he affirmed, is holy and one; the Visible Church is imperfect and divided (Smith n.d.).

By these and similar intellectual devices the existence of a divided Church was rationalized and the denominational system became the developmental pattern for Protestantism. Although the "established" churches made a noble effort during the latter part of the sixteenth and through the seventeenth centuries to curb "enthusiasm" and enforce conformity, they were unable to prevent the rise of independent movements and "sectaries." During the eighteenth and nineteenth centuries proliferation accelerated, especially in America, and the already sundered "body of Christ" exploded into hundreds of fragments. The dawn of the twentieth century saw Christian rivalry, accentuated competition, and proselytism rampant, and very few prophets to raise a voice against the scandal of division (Smith n.d.).

Then the mood began to change. The nineteenth century had also seen some great developments on the positive side. Most Protestant churches had shown unprecedented growth and expansion numerically, geographically, and programmatically. Missionary activity, though often competitive in the mood of the time, had extended Christian outposts to every continent and to remote islands in every sea. New program emphases, such as youth work, Sunday schools, and social service, began to appear in almost all the churches (Smith n.d.).

Although these programs often were used as new weapons in the denominational warfare, a different dimension of encounter emerged. Christians believers who would hardly speak to each other in their own communities were found sharing ideas. They communicated at Sunday school conventions and worked alongside each other in the city slums or on some far-off mission field. So as a result of backlash from missionary outreach and the byproducts of other grand ventures, many Christian leaders began to raise serious questions about the values of vicious and wasteful competition. Shortly after the turn of the century, suggestions were being made from many quarters regarding possibilities for dialogue and cooperation across denominational lines (Smith n.d.).

Consequently, after centuries of division and conflict, a great number of Christians in our time have come to the point of evidencing great concern about the divided condition of the Church and are trying to do something about it. The change in ecclesiastical climate is nothing short of phenomenal. Within the twentieth century, more attention has been directed toward healing the breaches in Christendom than in any other period since the major disruption of institutional unity in the sixteenth century.

Great world conferences have been held, interdenominational organizations have been constituted, ecumenical commissions have been created, hundreds of books have been published, numerous periodicals dealing entirely with ecumenicity have appeared, and the Vatican Council II has brought Roman Catholics as well as Protestants and Orthodox into the arena of ecumenical discussion and activity (Smith n.d.).

Seminaries, originally founded to provide a distinctive denominationally oriented ministry, are now cooperating and "clustering" with other schools, Protestant and Catholic, in order to provide a broadly ecumenical education for future leaders of the Church. Many denominational mergers have been successfully effected, and most religious bodies have created a department or commission whose specific assignment is to seek ways to promote Christian unit. To cite all contemporary activities which relate to seeking a solution to the problem of a divided Christendom would be very difficult, but if such were possible it would only accentuate the very apparent irenic climate among many of the presently constituted segments of the Church (Smith n.d.).

The question is now apparent of where the proponents of Holiness have stood—and are standing—in the midst of all this denominational competition and ecumenicity. Using a basically historical framework for analysis with concomitant theological and practical implications dealt with in context, six generalizations may be posited in regard to this issue. To avoid any accusation of bias, three of them point toward separateness and three point toward unity. All of them relate the Holiness emphasis as derived from Wesleyan theology to the problem of Christian disunity (Smith n.d.).

Holiness as a doctrinal emphasis has tended to be a divisive issue. Certainly there is nothing inherent in the doctrine of Holiness that would lead to separateness or division among Christians. On the theoretical face of it, quite the opposite would be true. Such terms as perfect love, Christian Perfection, and sanctification suggest anything but dissension and disunity. The fact of the matter is, as any student of the Holiness Movement knows well, holiness has been the topic for a considerable amount of bitter debate and man severed relationships. The "saints" not only have fought their adversaries; they also have battled each other. Even in an era when harsh polemics were in style, they often exhibited a pungent vocabulary of notable causticity and graphic castigation. Their deep commitment to the doctrine and their intense fervor in propagating it made Holiness people not only strong protagonists but also formidable adversaries (Smith n.d.).

The most specific manifestation of divisiveness fostered by the Holiness emphasis was in the separation of factions and the formation of new denominations. Although few groups would admit to intentional divisiveness, the fact remains that almost without exception the Holiness bodies came into being through schismatic action on the part of those who were vigorously upholding the doctrine in the face of opposition in the parent body (Smith n.d.).

Professors of Holiness should not voluntarily surrender their church privileges for trivial causes. But, if an oppressive hand be laid upon them in any case by Church authority, solely for professing Holiness, or for being identified with the cause of Holiness, and deprives them of the privileges of Christian communion, they should then adjust themselves to circumstances, as may be required in order to have the continued enjoyment of the ordinances of our holy religion (Smith n.d.).

Such separations, of course, were always the result of the "hard core of resistance" in the parent group rather than any lack of wisdom or charitableness on the part of the sanctified rebels. William M. Greathouse well describes the oft repeated process: "Increasingly, the people who had espoused the doctrine, which was never meant to be a theological provincialism, found themselves unwelcome in their parent denominations. With agapeic hesitancy, but with New Testament poignancy, they formed small denominations."

In reviewing the formation of this multitude of independent churches in the wake of the Holiness revival, Timothy L. Smith, in an excellent chapter entitled "The Church Question, 1880-1900," analyzes the complexity of factors, which produced this circumstance. He notes first that the Holiness emphasis found adherents among people from a wide variety of backgrounds, both religiously and culturally, so the movement itself was far from being homogeneous in character. Very early, a basic cleavage emerged between the rural and urban wings of the awakening, the former being more emotional and rigid in defining standards and the latter being more intellectual and flexible (Smith n.d.).

The Holiness Movement has been from its beginning and continues to be interdenominational in both theory and practice. It is not difficult to document the fact that the central leaders of the Holiness Movement never intended that the proponents of this doctrine should be confined to a single denomination. Although most of these leaders were Methodists, their vision of the field for the promotion of this work was as broad as the Christian faith itself. The official "call" to that first organizational camp meeting in Vineland, N.J., in 1867 makes the interdenominational emphasis doubly clear (Smith n.d.).

Another striking feature of the meeting was that so many Christian denominations were represented.

Presbyterians, Baptists, Episcopalians, Lutherans, Friends, and Methodists were all dwelling together in harmony. Never was there a more beautiful illustration of the Psalmist's declaration, "Behold how good and how pleasant it is for brethren to dwell together in unity!" (Psalms 133:1). One Presbyterian minister had come from Illinois to receive the baptism of fire, and he did receive it. A Baptist minister from Philadelphia came for the holy anointing, and the Spirit of power came upon him. He went to the Baptist church in Vineland on Sunday morning, preached to them on the text, "And the very God of peace sanctify you wholly," and held up to them distinctly the privilege of full salvation in the blood of the Lamb. All the later developments of Holiness associations – whether local, regional, or national – have stressed and continue to emphasize the interdenominational character of the movement. The focus of attention has been on the promotion of the doctrine and practice of Holiness and not on other affiliations which a person might have. Wide and diverse participation in all the associations was eagerly sought after because this broadened the potential field for promotion (Smith n.d.).

Although Holiness as a doctrine has been developed and advanced most specifically by those in the Arminian-Wesleyan tradition, and it never has been regarded by its proponents as private property of the Methodists. The teaching has been presented as biblical and Christian and available to all, regardless of their denomination. Holiness groups have tended to be aloof from general ecumenical activity. The massive ecumenical bustle of the twentieth century referred to earlier has developed largely without the encouragement or the assistance of Holiness-oriented leadership. Currently no avowedly Holiness body in the United States is a full member of the World Council of Churches. One, the Salvation Army, has held membership but is not listed on the 1974 roster. The British Salvation Army, however, does participate in the World Council. The National Council of Churches lists no Holiness churches in its membership, but five Arminian groups and one Canadian bod with Holiness orientation have been approved for participation in selected units of the Council's programmatic activity. The degree and extent of participation varied widely from group to group and from time to time (Smith n.d.).

If one were to attempt to analyze the reasons for this basically non-ecumenical stance, he/she would find it difficult to formulate any overall generalizations. As a result of the review, however, at least one factor is historically evident. Almost without exception the Holiness groups were born out of conflict with the very religious denominations that make up the mainline ecumenical organizations, thus creating an inherent, though often subconscious, reluctance to lock arms with one's former adversaries. Beyond this, there are the usual evangelical objections to cooperating with groups more "liberal" in theology and more "leftist" in politics. Pronouncements on social issues and involvement in protest activism have not been highly regarded by Holiness people as proper procedures for proclamation, albeit there is an evident heightening social concern among all Evangelicals. These theological and social issues would not apply, of course, to non-cooperation through the NAE. Here the reasons for aloofness would be less accusative and probably less specific. For some it is simple, while for others there are problems of attitude and spirit. Still others see all "conciliarism" as an abortive approach to true Christian unity, and so do not join any organization for this purpose (Smith n.d.).

Putting it all together, one must conclude that Holiness followers had not been highly enthusiastic about the promotion of unity through entering into associational relationships with a broad spectrum of other Christians throughout the nation or around the world.

Holiness has been promoted largely through cooperative "associational" measures and has also been the basis for some significant denominational mergers. The tendencies toward divisiveness and aloofness mentioned earlier have not subverted an even stronger inclination to devise was to identify with and establish vehicles of cooperation with others of like mind and spirit (Smith n.d.).

Holiness people have never been secluded. From the "class meetings" of the Wesley to the "Tuesday meetings" of the Palmers to the "camp meetings" of modern times, togetherness has been integral to the Holiness emphasis. This togetherness has never been incidental or casual; it has been deliberate and planned. From the earliest days of the movement, the proponents of this doctrine have joined together in trans-denominational associations, assemblies, and bands. These structures were conceived as completely non-ecclesiastical. Their function was solely for the promotion of Holiness, and no participant's denominational affiliation or loyalty was challenged (Smith n.d.).

To more effectively promote the spread of Holiness and unify the work of the kingdom, organizations of bands and county and state associations with uniformity of constitution and by-laws should come together. This Assembly, composed of members from at least twenty different evangelical churches, declares that these bands and associations are in no sense churches, were never intended to be churches, and are not to take the place of churches, but are simply a union of people for the promotion and conservation of Holiness. At various times throughout the history of the movement there have been those who have sought to unify the whole effort through some central coordinating agency. S. B. Shaw of Lansing, Michigan, for example, had a dream of forming a national Holiness union and was one of the promoters of the assemblies held in Chicago first in 1885 and again in 1901. He hoped that these assemblies would eventuate in just such a union, but it never developed that way (Smith n.d.).

The association idea did not die with the sectizing of Holiness, however, but it was forced to take a different focus. Since many participants were no longer members of the parent churches, they were not free to promote Holiness inside those walls, so more attention was given to the development of the new denominations and less attention to the associations. Man of the local and regional organizations dropped out of existence entirely, and the National Holiness Association itself went through some very lean years. Recent developments reflect new vigor, and the change in name to the Christian

Holiness Association opens the way to broaden both purpose and function (Smith n.d.). The strength of the cooperative impulse in Holiness people is reflected in the fact that hardly was the fragmenting process under way until the merging process began. Here again, the details are many and impressive, but they have been reviewed adequately elsewhere. It is sufficient here to note that, from the bringing together of five groups to form the Church of the Nazarene in 1895, to the recent mergers which have produced the Missionary church and the Wesleyan church, there has been evidenced a continuing urge to bring strength and unity to the cause of promoting Holiness. Even now conversations are in process to further unity and enhance this witness (Smith n.d.).

Holiness leaders generally have tended to give only marginal attention to the matter of Christian unity, have steadfastly defended the denomination system, and have disclaimed "come outism." The fact that Holiness people have been strongly associational does not mean they have been concerned about Christian unity. Their cooperation has been focused on a specific purpose, which is the promotion of Holiness, and has not been directed toward the overcoming of division and the unification of the Church. One might go even further and state that the central emphasis on personal holiness has so occupied the thought of leaders of the movement that little attention has been given even to articulating a doctrine of the Church, and much less to formulating concepts of the unity of the Church. This is not to say that a concern for the nature of the Church and its unity is entirely absent. One can examine a whole section of books on Holiness in a seminary library and find few which include any treatment of the "ecclesial" implications of the doctrine (Smith n.d.).

The deep concern on the part of early leaders of the movement that the Holiness emphasis should not be confined to a single religious group put them in the position of condoning, and seeking to work within, all existing groups. A Holiness preacher was not just a Holiness preacher; he was a Methodist, Baptist, or Presbyterian preacher who preached Holiness. As the associations were formed, there were usually specific stipulations that participants were to be "members in good standing" of some Christian denomination (Smith n.d.).

The development of religious events reveals that God intervenes in human history. He intervenes in history when He wills. After considering the total salvation accomplished by Christ the Redeemer, we would now like to reflect on its progressive realization in human history.

All times and seasons are governed by the Providence of God. Jesus' admonition concerning "God's times" proves more significant than ever after two thousand years of Christianity. As believers face the rather slow growth of God's kingdom in the world, they are asked to trust in the plan of the merciful Father who guides all things with transcendent wisdom. Jesus invites us to admire the "patience" of the Father, who adapts his transforming action to the slowness of human nature wounded by sin. This patience was already revealed in the Old Testament, in the long history which prepared Jesus' coming. It continues to be revealed after Christ, in the growth of his Church (II Peter 3:9.

The Holy Spirit worked new marvels of grace within religious history. The disciples could shrink from this demanding mission. They judge themselves incapable of assuming such a serious responsibility. Jesus shows them the secret that will enable them to fulfill this task: "You shall receive power when the Holy Spirit has come upon you" (Acts 1:8). With this power the disciples succeeded, despite human weakness, in being authentic witnesses of Christ throughout the world.

At Pentecost the Holy Spirit fills each of the disciples and the entire community with the abundance and diversity of his gifts. Jesus reveals the importance of the gift of power, which will sustain their apostolic work. The Holy Spirit came upon Mary at the Annunciation as the power of the Most High, bringing about the miracle of the Incarnation in her womb (Luke 1:35). The very power of the Holy Spirit will work new marvels of grace in the task of evangelizing the nations.

The example of the power of God in the lives of the disciples can be referenced as the same force that drove zealous religious explorers who pushed the message of Holiness across race and denominational lines. The Holiness agenda continues to impact religious doctrine and expansion across America and the world.

SUMMARY & CONCLUSION

The Holiness Movement was born out of a quest for deeper spiritual meaning and unresolved issues relating to believers' Christian walk with Jesus Christ. The breakout of Holiness preaching and teaching among mainline church organizations in the early nineteenth century was crucial in giving greater substance to religious culture in America.

John Wesley's beliefs regarding Entire Sanctification blazed the trail for continual controversy regarding the question of religious purity. Debate and differences over religious theology ignited the flame of curiosity that paved the way for the evolution of the American Holiness Movement.

John Wesley provided a valuable introduction to the place of the doctrine of Christian Perfection in American Methodism. The evidence he presents makes clear that from its establishment in 1784 to the first decade of the nineteenth century the Methodist Church was firmly committed to the proclamation of full salvation. With Wesley's strong encouragement, the leadership of the newly founded church was determined to make Entire Sanctification an important doctrinal emphasis. It was apparent that the preaching of "holiness of heart" was particularly prominent just after the turn of the century.

The theology of Holiness thought is based on the fact that Holiness is the state or quality of being holy. God requires all believers to be holy (Lev. 20: 7). The God of the Bible is the very essence and source of that which is holy. Three attributes demonstrating that God is holy are: (1) the fact that He is morally pure and always speaks the truth. (2) God is righteous, meaning that he always acts in a manner that is just. Because God is righteous and just, He cannot overlook sin, and He must punish wrong. (3) However, God is merciful, and, in his great love for humanity, wanted to give people a chance to avoid eternal punishment. By allowing His son. Jesus Christ to suffer punishment for our sins, God can justly forgive sinners who repent of their sins and accept Jesus Christ as the Lord of their life (I John 1: 9-10). When a believer lives in a manner consistent with the divine will of God, that person is in a state of being holy. God requires His people to live a life of Holiness (Hebrews 12:14).

Holiness theology was the bridge that facilitated a process leading to the doctrine of American Pentecostalism. Man of the Pentecostal followers were members of Holiness groups prior to becoming part of the Pentecostal church. The main difference separating the two doctrines was the gifts of the Holy Spirit. Even today Holiness and Pentecostal churches can be considered siblings. The Holiness church has a prominent place in religious history because it was the catalyst that encouraged religious beliefs that evolved into many different church organizations across America.

American Pentecostalism is made up of many diverse organizations, some of which are predominantly southern in membership and influence. Much of the drama of the early Pentecostal church occurred in the South, where Holiness Movements had intermittently swept the area for decades. In 1901, Charles Parham, a Kansas Holiness preacher, laid the doctrinal and experimental foundations of the modern Pentecostal Movement. The Movement grew for five years, primarily in Kansas, Oklahoma, and Texas, until 1906 when William Seymour took the message to California. At a warehouse on Azusa Street in Los Angeles, the distinctive Pentecostal assertion spread and shaped a movement that would have long-term significance for American religion especially in the South.

The Pentecostal Movement in America evolved from the closely preceding Holiness Movement, which itself was established from the much earlier Wesleyan emphasis on experiencing Christian Perfection after redemption. At the end of the nineteenth century and the beginning of the twentieth, many individuals and groups of people withdrew from established religious organizations to escape what they perceived as liberalism, modernism, and worldliness. By 1906, some outspoken southern Holiness advocates had left their original base in the Methodist Episcopal Church and formed independent groups, some of which had developed precise definitions of valid spiritual experience and appropriate Christian behavior. Prohibitions against pork, coffee, soft drinks, chewing gum, tobacco, spectator sports, alcohol, dancing, and mixed bathing as well as directives regarding jewelry, hair styles, and types of clothing were common.

The Pentecostal Movement represented a theological division within the Holiness Movement. This division was the result of a controversy over the evidence required to prove that a believer had been baptized with the Holy Spirit. The Pentecostals held the belief that glossolalia, or speaking in tongues, was always the initial evidence of a religious experience indicating baptism by the Holy Spirit. The baptism is usually an ecstatic experience that is sometimes characterized by dancing, shouting, and convulsive movements. It also consists of running in the Spirit (running around the sanctuary), and rolling on the floor. Those churches, which did not accept this interpretation, continued in the classical Holiness Movement, while the Pentecostals split off and developed different modes of worship and different theological interpretations. Essentially, however, the Pentecostal Movement began as somewhat more of an emotional and theologically experimental branch of the Holiness Movement, and continued to practice these beliefs.

The experiences witnessed at Azusa Street caused many followers of the Holiness faith to leave their original beliefs and form other religious groups. Thousands of pilgrims, curious about and hungry for what Seymour claimed to offer, poured down Azusa Street between 1906 and 1909. But while the Azusa Street Revival weathered the external storm of criticism, it soon began to unravel internally. Religious leaders disagreed on points of the experience and some never reconciled.

Shockwaves also came over racial tension. In the early months of Azusa Street, blacks, whites, men, and women, shared leadership, although African Americans were the majority. But soon Seymour asked all the Hispanics to leave, and eventually wrote by-laws that prevented anyone except African-Americans from holding office. By 1909, the revival was spent and eventually faded into history. Even the mission building was razed after Seymour's death.

However, even as the Azusa Street Revival's tires died out, a movement had ignited that would not die. Pentecostalism had spread all over the world. Denominations such as the Assemblies of God and the United Pentecostal Church had been formed, and a large segment of the American church would forever view Azusa Street as the high watermark of modern Christianity. The Pentecostal Movement was a focal point for change and diversification of many religious disciplines.

A confusion as to the distinction between Holiness and Pentecostal groups persists to the present time, and is exacerbated by the fact that in actual practice the lines distinguishing the two groups have been substantially blurred. So far as some believers are concerned there is no distinction, for these groups embrace both the requirements of conversion and holiness or sanctification as prerequisite for salvation as well as the third work of grace called the baptism in the Holy Ghost, which is manifested in glossolalia of speaking in tongues (Lincoln C. and Lawrence M. 1990).

The impact of Holiness doctrine was the foundation for change and the stratification of many religious organizations across America. All across America the Holiness revival is being reborn. Many churches are becoming more fervent about Holiness doctrine. Religious leaders are talking about Holiness. Open debate about doctrinal issues is being replaced by honest and open self-examination. There are serious discussions about the future of the Movement among leaders. Holiness groups are in a private oft-the-record process of self-definition. They are asking themselves who they really are and what they will stand for.

The Holiness Movement has evolved and is continuing to evolve into new religious denominations. Many worship styles and doctrines can be traced back to Holiness and Pentecostal roots. Renewed interest in the Holiness cause should encourage all followers of Holiness teaching. Believers should be encouraged because biblical truth always resurfaces. The Holiness message is alive. Holiness is pervasive in the Bible. God called a holy nation, set aside a holy priesthood, established a holy Sabbath, and prescribed only holy sacrifices to be done on a holy mount in a holy Temple with a holy place, even a Holy of Holies.

ENDNOTES

1. Primary doctrinal emphasis is on Entire Sanctification, by which believers are freed from original sin and brought into a state of entire devotement to God. The church's government is representative, with balance between ministerial and lay membership on administrative boards. The doctrine of Entire Sanctification is the teaching that led to the establishment of many religious denominations in the United States and in the world.

2. The Alsatian Lutheran Pastor Johann Friedrich is known for his philanthropic efforts and educational innovations. Educated at Strasbourg, he was pastor of Waldersbach, Ban-de-Roche, in the Vosges from 1767 until his death. Influenced both by the enlightenment ideas of Jean Jaques Rousseau and by the Christian Mysticism of Emanuel Von Swedenborg, he promoted engineering, agricultural, and educational reforms within his parish. His work eventually won international recognition, especially his principles of infant education, as developed by Johann Pestalozzi. The Oberlin House was located in Potsdam, Germany. His theology and ideas are known as the Oberlin Theology.

3. Holiness churches are united in the belief that Christians can approach freedom from sin during their earthly lives. In addition to one's baptism into the Christian faith, Holiness churches teach that the Second Blessing, a baptism of the Holy Spirit, makes perfect the Christian impulse toward moral sanctification. Strong belief in the power of the Holy Spirit often means that Holiness services are enthusiastic occasions for worship.

4. Speaking in tongues (Glossolalia) is a Christian phenomenon in which the believer, in an ecstatic state, speaks in a foreign language or utters unintelligible sounds that are taken to contain a divine message. Many Christians believe the genuine gifts of tongues were confined to earliest Christianity, at Pentecost, and during conversion experiences. Modern revivalist movements such as the Pentacostalists and Charismatics believe it to be given in contemporary times as a testimony to the special presence of the Holy Spirit.

5. Protestantism is a movement in western Christianity whose adherents reject the notion that divine authority is channeled through a particular human institution or person such as the Roman Catholic pope. It is the idea that people are saved by grace through faith in Jesus Christ. Protestants look elsewhere for the authority of their faith. Most of them look to the Bible as the source and the norm of their teaching.

6. Lutheranism soon became more than the experience of Luther, but it never deviated from his theme that people are made right with God sola gratia and sola fide, only by the divine initiative of grace as received through God's gift of faith. Because Luther came across his discoveries by reading be Bible, he also liked to

add to his motto the exhortation sola scriptura, which means that Lutherans are to use the Bible alone as the source and norm for their teachings.

7. The Azusa Street Movement is a title given to a fellowship of Holiness groups who conducted a five week revival at Azusa Street. The event was crucial to religious history because it was significant to the birth of Pentecostalism. After experiencing Spirit baptism and speaking in tongues, many of the leaders of the groups took the testimony of the experience back to their churches. The worship practice divided many leaders and stratified the religious groups into several denominations.

8. The removal of sin or to place the fault or guilt on someone else is renunciation, the act of renouncing the sin in one's life and embracing a life of righteousness. Atonement has reference to the reconciliation of man back to fellowship with God the Father.

BIBLIOGRAPHY

Bassett, P. M. (2001). The Holiness Movement and the Protestant Principle [Online].
Avail-able: http://wesley.nnu.edu/theojrnl/16-20/18-01.htm

Brown, C. E. (1997). Pentecostalism [Online].
Available: http://religiousmovements.lib.virginia.edu/nrms/penta.html

Buckley, J. M. (1898). A History of Methodism in the United States. New York: Harper & Brothers. Cobbins, O. B. (1966). History of Church of Christ Holiness U.S.A., 1895-1965. New York: Vantage Press.

Fagan, P. F. (1996). Why religion matters: The Impact of Religious Practices on Social Stability [Online]
Available: htt://christianparty.net/mdfagan.htm

Glock, C. Y. & Bellah, R. N. (Eds.). (1976). The New Religious Consciousness. Berkeley, CA: University of California Press.

Hocking, W. E. (1912). The Meaning of God in Human Experience: A Philosophic Study of Religion. New Haven: Yale University Press.

Hollenweger, W. E. (1988). The Pentecostals. Peabody, AA: Hendrickson.

Lincoln, C. Eric, and Lawrence Mamiya. (1990) The Black Church in the African American Experience. Durham, N. C.: Duke University Press

Longman, R. Jr. (2001a,). Azusa street timeline [Online].
Available: http://www.spirithome.com/hist-pen1.html

Longman, R. Jr. (2001b,). Pre-Pentecostal History [Online].
Available: http://www.spirithome.com/histpent.html

Longman, R. Jr. (2001e,). Pentecostalism after Azusa: Some historical notes [Online].
Available: http://www.spirithome.com/histpen2.html

Moltmann, J. (1993) Pentecostal Movements as a Ecumenical Challenge [Online].
http://www.concilium.org/english/intro963.htm

Owen, C. H. (1988). The Sacred Flame of Love: Methodism and Society in Nineteenth Century Georgia.

Athens, GA: University of Georgia Press.

Pierard, R.V. (2001). American Holiness Movement: Advanced Information [Online].
Available: http://www.mb-soft.com/believe/text/holiness.htm

Posey, W. B. (1933). The Development of Methodism in the Old Southwest, 1783-1824 (Thesis, Vanderbilt University, 1933).

Rice, H. (1975). The Gift and Gifts of the Holy Spirit [Online]. Available: http://www.brfwitness.org/Articles/1975v10n1.htm

Robbins, D. A. (1995) Understanding Spiritual Gifts. [Online]. Available: http://www.victorious.ord/sprgifts.htm

Sanders, C. J. (1996). Saints in Exile: The Holiness-Pentecostal Experience in African American Religion and Culture. New York: Oxford University Press.

Slade, J. A. (n.d.) The "Pentecostal" Movement and the Jesus Revolution. [Online] Available: http://www.presenttruthmag.com/archive/I-3.htm

Smith, T. L. (1962). Called unto Holiness: The story of the Nazarenes: The Formative Years. Kansas City, MO: Nazarene Publishing.

Smith, W.V. (n.d.) Holiness and Unity [Online] Available http://wesley.nnuedu/theojrn1/06-10/10-3.htm

Synan, V. (2001). The Origins of the Pentecostal Movement [Online]. Available: http://www.oru.edu/university/library/holy spirit/pentorg1.html

Warfield, B. (1990). Entire Sanctification (Online]. Available: http://www.markers.com/ink/bbwentire.htm

To order additional copies of
The Holiness Experience and Its Evolution

Please visit our web site at www.pleasantword.com

Also available at: www.amazon.com
and
www.barnesandnoble.com

www.ingramcontent.com/pod-product-compliance
Lightning Source LLC
LaVergne TN
LVHW092051060526
838201LV00047B/1342